A CROCHET WORLD
of Creepy Creatures and Cryptids

A CROCHET WORLD

of Creepy Creatures *and* Cryptids

40
Amigurumi Patterns for Adorable Monsters,
Mythical Beings and More

Rikki Gustafson

Founder of Crocheted by Rikki

PAGE STREET
PUBLISHING CO.

PAGE STREET
PUBLISHING CO.

Copyright © 2022 Rikki Gustafson

First published in 2022 by
Page Street Publishing Co.
27 Congress Street, Suite 1511
Salem, MA 01970
www.pagestreetpublishing.com

Distributed by Macmillan, sales in Canada by The Canadian Manda Group.

26   25   24   23   4   5   6

ISBN-13: 978-1-64567-538-9
ISBN-10: 1-64567-538-6

Library of Congress Control Number: 2021952287

Cover and book design by Laura Benton for Page Street Publishing Co.
Photography by Becca Blevins

Printed and bound in the United States

Page Street Publishing protects our planet by donating to nonprofits like The Trustees, which focuses on local land conservation.

This book is dedicated to anyone who is going through a
hard time. The first time I picked up a hook was during a very
difficult period, and I want you to know it changed my life.
I haven't put it down since, and I have never felt better.
I hope that the patterns in this book will help you feel
uplifted and empowered in your creativity.

TABLE OF CONTENTS

INTRODUCTION

Hello, friends!

I cannot tell you how excited I am that you have picked up this book. I poured my heart and soul into these designs and couldn't be more thrilled to share them with you! There are *40* amigurumi patterns in here! Most crochet books have twenty patterns or less, so that should tell you there really is something special in the pages to come. My goal was to make a book that didn't have simple little patterns for simple little things. I wanted you to be able to make really, really cool things—things that no one has crocheted before. It was a challenge to make these incredibly complicated and grotesque creatures into something that anyone could crochet, and I am happy to report it is done!

I researched these creatures extensively by studying what lore told us they look like, then I figured out how to make them in my own style. If you look at reference pictures, you will find out pretty quickly that these are complicated and often unsightly creatures. I did my absolute best to make them cute, chibi and endearing; that way even the most horrendous of creatures would make people say *aww* when they saw it made out of yarn!

If you are unfamiliar with me or my work, all you need to know is that my passion is making things that people will cherish forever. I feel that's what I was put on this earth to do, and I hope that these patterns can help you make things for others (or yourself!) that will be cherished for lifetimes to come. When you finish a project from this book, I would love if you'd share your finished project using #creaturesandcryptids on Instagram so we can connect!

Happy crocheting!

Rikki

Rikki Gustafson

TECHNIQUES

In the following sections, I will talk about some important techniques I use quite often. These techniques include tension, using different yarns and painting eyes. If you are a total crochet pro, you can likely skip the next section on tension. However, if you saw the word "tension" and you're not entirely sure what I mean, if you are intrigued by using different yarns or if you have always wondered how crocheters are getting uniquely colored eyes for their dolls, then this section is for you! I have been crocheting for quite some time, and I am *always* striving to learn new techniques. I am a firm believer in finding ways to improve my dolls. I hope you find the following information helpful as you continue your crochet journey!

Tension

Tension in crochet means how tight your stitches are. Tension is very important when making garments, but it is *not* as important when making plushies. No two people crochet the same, and that is what makes all of our dolls so unique to us. It is not necessary to create a swatch to match gauge when making these dolls, which is why there is no mention of gauge in this book.

The only thing I want to specifically mention about tension is that I crochet *very* tightly. My dolls come out smaller than others, because of this. Therefore, when I am using a 9mm safety eye, it looks proportionate to *my* plushie's head. But, if *you* do not crochet as tightly (which is completely fine because it is your own style, just like this is mine!), and you use a 9mm eye, it may appear to be too small for the head you made. The solution would be to scale your eye size up to a 12mm eye (or greater depending on your tension) despite the pattern calling for 9mm. You may find the larger eye is much more proportionate for your piece! There is no wrong way to make these dolls; there is no tension that is better than others. We all have our own style, and it is so fun to see your skills develop over time. This is just a little piece of advice to consider if you find that our tensions are vastly different! However, if you are seeing your stuffing coming through your stitches, that's an issue with tension and you might want to consider adjusting it to be slightly tighter.

Jumbo Plushies!!!

Let's talk about BIG YARN! Big yarns—such as blanket yarns, velvet or chenille or even double-stranding medium worsted yarn—have become increasingly popular for making plushies. Let's face it: Big dolls are fun! And even better, big yarn doesn't require as tight of stitches as dolls made out of medium worsted weight yarn! Sometimes small stitches can hurt hands, and it breaks my heart when I hear that people have to stop crocheting because their hands hurt too much when they do.

I'm going to let you in on a secret: Any amigurumi pattern can be done in big, textured yarn. That's right, all it takes is knowing what hook to use and scaling your eyes up! Every single pattern in this book can be made with thicker yarn. You will get a much bigger doll, but guess what? Your hands won't hurt if you usually suffer when using small hooks! Sometimes even I need a break from crocheting so tightly, and so I crochet with blanket yarn and a big hook to give my hands a break.

Most of the time when working with medium worsted weight yarn (just your average run-of-the-mill acrylic) I use a 4.0mm hook and between 6mm to 15mm safety eyes (depending on the project). When I want to scale up and use standard velvet yarn, I use a 5.5mm hook and 12 to 18mm safety eyes (depending on the project). When I use blanket yarn, I use between a 6.0 to 7.0mm hook and anywhere from 20mm to 30mm eyes.

The bigger the hook size, the bigger your doll will become, and the bigger eyes you will need. Be careful, though; if you go too big, your stitches my start to have gaps and stuffing may show. I personally prefer my dolls to have very small gaps and never have stuffing showing, hence the very tight stitches and why I still stay on the smaller side of hooks even when using bigger yarn.

Don't be afraid to explore different yarns and hook sizes and find not only what works for you, but what you find most fun! Don't be discouraged or think you can't swap yarns just because a pattern specifies something. Crocheting is so much fun. When you try new things, you learn; and when you learn, you improve your work. Watching your own progress is one of the neatest things!

Painting Eyes

In this book I used several different colors of safety eyes. If you're like me from a couple of years ago, you may be wondering where the heck I got them from! Well this section is for you—I painted them!

When I first started out, I had no idea that could even be done! I saw all these beautiful amigurumis with glittery purple eyes or scary red eyes, and I thought about how cool it would be to have some of those for my own dolls. I started painting my eyes for special dolls just a couple years ago, and I tried *a lot* of different techniques. The one I found best is described here:

First, obtain your desired size of plain black safety eyes. Gather a scrap piece of cardboard, and puncture 2 small holes in it; insert your safety eye posts into those holes. *Do not press your safety eye all the way down, but leave it sticking up so that as you paint, it does not get stuck to the cardboard!*

Next, you will need 2 colors of spray paint: white and the color you would like your eye to be. You'll paint a white base coat so the next layer will pop. If you are coloring your eyes with a light color, it may not pop as much or will need more coats to look vibrant if you did not include the white base coat. There are so many colors and textures of spray paint out there, the possibilities are endless! (Obviously, if you just want white eyes, you only need 1 color!) Start with a base coat of just white spray paint. Spray both eyes evenly with a thin layer, then *allow it to dry*! Once they are dry, do another layer of white paint. If your eyes are looking pretty vibrantly white, no additional layers are needed of the base coat. If they are still

looking kind of splotchy, wait for each layer to dry, then add more layers until the eyes are smooth and vibrant.

Once your base coat is completely dry, it's time to use the real color! Spray very thin layers; you don't want puddles of liquid forming as you spray, because they will drip and not look as smooth as they could. Always wait until the previous layer is dry before adding the next. Add as many layers as it takes for your top coat to be as vibrant as you'd like; I usually do about three, depending on the brand of spray paint I am using. Then you should wait a minimum of 1 hour for the paint to dry, but it could take up to 8 hours depending on the product you used. Once the eyes are dry, you can go ahead and insert them in your amigurumi; now you've got an awesome piece of detail!

Safety Note: The dolls I make are intended for adult collectors. Some of my customers gift these dolls to children, but I always remind them to do so at their own risk. Painted eyes may be dangerous to young recipients who may try to consume the paint. The packaging on safety eyes states they are not intended for children under 3. However, they are pretty darn secure. For example, if I seal a safety eye but made a placement mistake, I have to throw the whole piece away because there is no way to get it off! So please use your best judgment when gifting these dolls to children.

Chapter 1

CRYPTIDS

The great debate that has spanned over lifetimes, continents and cultures . . . are cryptids real?! The evidence may not be as substantial as some skeptics would like, but hey, it was enough for me to design these elusive creatures for you. In the following chapter, we will work our way through some of the biggest names out there! Mothman (page 23), Nessie (page 19) and even the Chupacabra (page 25), just to name a few. Take a closer look and maybe when you hold them in your hand, you'll be swayed to believe in them a little more than you did before!

CTHULHU

Perhaps the oldest and strongest cryptid of them all is Cthulhu! He is not from our world; he is a deity from another dimension! As he is so much stronger and older than anything our world has ever seen, it is said that we puny mortals couldn't even begin to understand him and may even go mad if we gaze upon him. Cthulhu is referred to as the "Great Old One" and has inspired countless stories, games, movies and other monsters. Currently, Cthulhu is said to be hibernating in a lost city beneath the South Pacific Ocean. Enjoy making your very own Great Old One!

Materials Needed

- 4.0mm crochet hook (G hook)
- 1 (7-oz [198-g]) skein of medium worsted yarn in dark green (I used Caron's® Simply Soft® Dark Sage)
- 1 pair of 9mm safety eyes
- Fiberfill, for stuffing
- Tapestry needle
- Pins, to hold the limbs in place as you sew
- Scissors

Abbreviations

ch–chain

dec–invisible decrease

F/o–fasten off

HDC–half double crochet

inc–increase or 2 single crochets in the same stitch

mc–magic circle

sc–single crochet

Head

Round 1: mc 6. (6)

Round 2: (inc) 6 times. (12)

Round 3: (sc, inc) 6 times. (18)

Round 4: (2 sc, inc) 6 times. (24)

Round 5: (3 sc, inc) 6 times. (30)

Rounds 6–11: sc around. (30)

Round 12: (4 sc, inc) 6 times. (36)

In the next round, we will be making the tentacles; take your time and read the pattern carefully, and don't feel discouraged if you have to try a couple of times to get it right!

Round 13: 6 sc, (ch 12, HDC in each chain, starting in the second chain from the hook, sc into the next stitch of the head) 4 times, 26 sc. (36)

In Round 14, you will sc around the head. When you get to the tentacles, you will put a sc under each tentacle (creating a stitch) and a sc in between each tentacle (where the sc from the previous row exists). This is how we go from having these 4 stitches, hosting 4 tentacles, to having 8 stitches in the front. We do this so the plush doesn't have big holes right under the tentacles. Do not stress if you don't have exactly 40 stitches after this row. It is the trickiest part of making this doll. If you have 39 or 41 stitches, that is just fine. All we're doing from here on out is decreasing!

Round 14: sc around. (~40)

Round 15: (8 sc, dec) 4 times. (~36)

Round 16: (4 sc, dec) 6 times. (~30)

Round 17: (3 sc, dec) 6 times. (~24)

(continued)

CTHULHU (CONTINUED)

Place the eyes between Rounds 11 and 12 with 5 stitches in between. Position the eyes so the tentacles are centered between them. Stuff the head firmly as you continue to decrease.

Round 18: (2 sc, dec) 6 times. (~18)

Round 19: (sc, dec) 6 times. (~12)

Round 20: (dec) 6 times. (~6)

F/o.

Body

Starting with the first leg

Round 1: mc 6. (6)

Round 2: (inc) 6 times. (12)

Rounds 3–7: sc around. (12)

F/o.

Second leg

Round 1: mc 6. (6)

Round 2: (inc) 6 times. (12)

Rounds 3–7: sc around. (12)

Do not fasten off; join the next stitch into the first leg, and consider this the first stitch of Round 8.

Round 8: sc around. (24)

Rounds 9–15: sc around. (24)

Round 16: (2 sc, dec) 6 times. (18)

Round 17: sc around. (18)

Round 18: (sc, dec) 6 times. (12)

F/o, leaving a long tail for sewing.

Arms—Make 2

Round 1: mc 6. (6)

Round 2: (sc, inc) 3 times. (9)

Rounds 3–9: sc around. (9)

F/o, leaving a long tail for sewing.

Wings—Make 2

The wings are made in rows, not rounds. Please read the pattern carefully.

Row 1: ch 5, turn.

Row 2: Start in the second chain from hook, 4 sc, ch 4 and turn.

Row 3: Start in the second chain from hook, 7 sc, ch 1 and turn.

Row 4: Start in the second chain from hook, 4 sc, ch 4 and turn.

Row 5: Start in the second chain from hook, 7 sc, ch 3 and turn.

Row 6: Start in the second chain from hook, 6 sc, ch 4 and turn.

Row 7: Start in the second chain from hook, 9 sc, do not chain or turn.

Row 8: sc around the top of the wing (you will be creating evenly spaced stitches along this ridge).

F/o, leaving a long tail for sewing.

Assembly

First, whipstitch the head closed. Next, stuff the body firmly and attach to the head. Pin the arms on either side of the torso and sew them on (no need to stuff them). Flip your Cthulhu around, and pin the wings to his back in whatever position you would like them to be in. Sew them on when you are happy with their placement. Use the scissors to cut any leftover yarn tails from the limbs you've attached. Give the tentacles a twist so they are nice and curly, and your Cthulhu is finished!

NESSIE

The Loch Ness Monster, more affectionately referred to as "Nessie," is probably the most famous cryptid of all! Said to reside in Loch Ness (located in the Scottish Highlands) since ancient times, she is a giant long-necked "sea monster" that pokes her head up out of the water every once in a while; she has rocked the modern world since alleged photos of her existence were shared in the 1930s. Though the evidence is widely disputed, there is something to say about how many tourists flock to this location every year in hopes of spotting her. Interestingly, there are also carvings depicting her on ancient Scottish stones found in the area! Believer or not, she is adorable, and now you can crochet your own little version of her!

Materials Needed

- 4.0mm crochet hook (G hook)
- 1 (7-oz [198-g]) skein of medium worsted yarn in green (I used Red Heart's® Super Saver® Paddy Green)
- 1 pair of 9mm safety eyes
- Fiberfill, for stuffing
- Tapestry needle
- Pins, to hold the limbs in place as you sew
- Scissors

Abbreviations

dec–invisible decrease

F/o–fasten off

inc–increase or 2 single crochets in the same stitch

mc–magic circle

sc–single crochet

Head

Round 1: mc 6. (6)

Round 2: (inc) 6 times. (12)

Round 3: sc around. (12)

Round 4: 4 sc, (inc) 4 times, 4 sc. (16)

Round 5: 6 sc, (inc) 4 times, 6 sc. (20)

Rounds 6–11: sc around. (20)

Round 12: (3 sc, dec) 4 times. (16)

Round 13: sc around. (16)

Insert the eyes between Rounds 4 and 5 with 5 stitches between them. Stuff the head firmly as you decrease.

Round 14: (2 sc, dec) 4 times. (12)

Round 15: (sc, dec) 4 times. (8)

Round 16: (dec) 4 times. (4)

F/o.

Front Half of Body/Neck

Round 1: mc 6. (6)

Round 2: (inc) 6 times. (12)

Round 3: (sc, inc) 6 times. (18)

Round 4: (2 sc, inc) 6 times. (24)

Rounds 5–8: sc around. (24)

Round 9: (2 sc, dec) 6 times. (18)

Round 10: (3 sc, dec) 3 times. (15)

Rounds 11–12: sc around. (15)

Round 13: (3 sc, dec) 3 times. (12)

Rounds 14–15: sc around. (12)

F/o, leaving a long tail for sewing.

(continued)

NESSIE (CONTINUED)

Back Half of Body

Round 1: mc 6. (6)

Round 2: (inc) 6 times. (12)

Round 3: (sc, inc) 6 times. (18)

Round 4: (2 sc inc) 6 times. (24)

Rounds 5–6: sc around. (24)

Round 7: (2 sc, dec) 6 times. (18)

Rounds 8–10: sc around. (18)

F/o, leaving a long tail for sewing.

Tail

Round 1: mc 6. (6)

Round 2: sc around. (6)

Round 3: (2 sc, inc) 2 times. (8)

Round 4: sc around. (8)

Round 5: (3 sc, inc) 2 times. (10)

Round 6: sc around. (10)

Round 7: (4 sc, inc) 2 times. (12)

Round 8: sc around. (12)

Round 9: (3 sc, inc) 3 times. (15)

Round 10: sc around. (15)

Round 11: (4 sc, inc) 3 times. (18)

Rounds 12–13: sc around. (18)

F/o, leaving a long tail for sewing.

Fins—Make 4

Round 1: mc 4. (4)

Round 2: (sc, inc) 2 times. (6)

Round 3: (2 sc, inc) 2 times. (8)

Round 4: (3 sc, inc) 2 times. (10)

Round 5: (4 sc, inc) 2 times. (12)

Rounds 6–7: sc around. (12)

Round 8: (dec) 6 times. (6)

F/o, leaving a long tail for sewing.

Assembly

Whipstitch the head closed, then stuff the front half of the body/neck firmly and sew it on the bottom of the head. Stuff the back half of the body piece firmly, and attach it to the back of the front half. Make sure you sew very tightly to make this connection as seamless as possible. Next, stuff the tail and attach it to the back of the back half of the body, making sure, once again, that you are pulling as tight as you can so that the connection is smooth. Pin the fins to the body, and play around with their positioning to help make sure the body is balanced and can stand up on its own (no need to stuff them). When you are happy with the positioning of the fins, sew them on. Use the scissors to cut any leftover yarn tails from the limbs you've attached. And with that, your Nessie is finished!

MOTHMAN

Mothman is a large, flying, shadowy creature. The first reported sightings of him were in a small town in West Virginia in 1966. He was spotted many times over the next year leading up to a tragic disaster that took place in 1967. After the event, he disappeared, and sightings have halted almost completely. Legend says that Mothman appears as an omen; if he is seen, consider it a warning that a disaster may soon follow! I have created a chibi (and hopefully non-scary) Mothman! You can hold a prophetic cryptid yourself or add it to any fan's collection!

Head/Body

In worsted black

Round 1: mc 6. (6)

Round 2: (inc) 6 times. (12)

Round 3: (sc, inc) 6 times. (18)

Round 4: (2 sc, inc) 6 times. (24)

Round 5: (3 sc, inc) 6 times. (30)

Round 6: (4 sc, inc) 6 times. (36)

Round 7: (5 sc, inc) 6 times. (42)

Rounds 8–20: sc around. (42)

Insert the eyes between Rounds 12 and 13 with 7 stitches between them. Stuff the head/body firmly as you decrease.

Round 21: (5 sc, dec) 6 times. (36)

Round 22: sc around. (36)

Round 23: (4 sc, dec) 6 times. (30)

Round 24: (3 sc, dec) 6 times. (24)

Round 25: (2 sc, dec) 6 times. (18)

Round 26: (sc, dec) 6 times. (12)

Round 27: (dec) 6 times. (6)

F/o.

Feet—Make 2

Round 1: mc 6. (6)

Round 2: (inc) 6 times. (12)

Rounds 3–5: sc around. (12)

F/o, leaving a long tail for sewing.

Arms—Make 2

Round 1: mc 6. (6)

Round 2: (sc, inc) 3 times. (9)

Rounds 3–6: sc around. (9)

F/o, leaving a long tail for sewing.

(continued)

Materials Needed

- 4.0mm crochet hook (G hook)
- 1 (7-oz [198-g]) skein of medium worsted yarn in black (I used Red Heart's Super Saver Black)
- 1 (10-oz [283-g]) skein of velvet yarn in black (I used Bernat® Velvet™ Blackbird)
- 1 pair of 12mm safety eyes (painted red as specified on page 13)
- Fiberfill, for stuffing
- Tapestry needle
- Pins, to hold the limbs in place as you sew
- Scissors

Abbreviations

ch—chain

dec—invisible decrease

F/o—fasten off

inc—increase or 2 single crochets in the same stitch

mc—magic circle

sc—single crochet

MOTHMAN (CONTINUED)

Antennae–Make 2

Round 1: mc 6. (6)

Round 2: (2 sc, inc) 2 times. (8)

Round 3: (3 sc, inc) 2 times. (10)

Round 4: (4 sc, inc) 2 times. (12)

Rounds 5–6: sc around. (12)

Round 7: (4 sc, dec) 2 times. (10)

Round 8: (3 sc, dec) 2 times. (8)

Wings–Make 2

The wings are made in rows, not rounds. Please read the pattern carefully.

In black velvet

Row 1: ch 5, turn.

Row 2: Start in the second chain from hook, 4 sc, ch 4 and turn.

Row 3: Start in the second chain from hook, 7 sc, ch 1 and turn.

Row 4: Start in the second chain from hook, 4 sc, ch 4 and turn.

Row 5: Start in the second chain from hook, 7 sc, ch 3 and turn.

Row 6: Start in the second chain from hook, 6 sc, ch 4 and turn.

Row 7: Start in the second chain from hook, 9 sc, do not chain or turn.

Row 8: sc around the top of the wing (you will be creating evenly spaced stitches along this ridge).

F/o, leaving a long tail for sewing.

Assembly

First, whipstitch the head/body closed. Stuff the feet and attach them to the bottom of the body. (Check to make sure your Mothman can sit up evenly before completely attaching both; these will be the only helpers in giving your doll balance!) Pin the arms to either side of the body and sew them on (no need to stuff them). Pin the wings to the back of your doll, and sew them on when you are happy with the placement. Finally, sew the antennae to the top of the head (no need to stuff these). Use the scissors to cut any leftover yarn tails from the limbs you've attached.

CHUPACABRA

Chupacabras are legendary creatures that live mostly throughout Latin America. They are considered vampire-esque, as they suck the blood from their prey, which mostly consists of farm animals they have easy access to in the night, but they do have a particular affinity for goats—to the horror of countless goat farmers! Chupacabras are scaly and have large fangs and sharp spikes going down their spines. They are reported to look like sickly, hairless coyotes. Doesn't sound very cute . . . so, I took some artistic liberties and did my best to create us a fun and precious version!

Materials Needed

- 4.0mm crochet hook (G hook)
- 1 (7-oz [198-g]) skein of medium worsted yarn in light green (I used Red Heart's Super Saver Frosty Green)
- 1 (7-oz [198-g]) skein of medium worsted yarn in white (I used Red Heart's Super Saver White)
- 1 pair of 12mm safety eyes
- Fiberfill, for stuffing
- Tapestry needle
- Pins, to hold the limbs in place as you sew
- Scissors

Abbreviations

ch–chain
DC–double crochet
dec–invisible decrease
F/o–fasten off
HDC–half double crochet
inc–increase or 2 single crochets in the same stitch
mc–magic circle
sc–single crochet
slpst–slip stitch

Head

In light green

Round 1: mc 6. (6)

Round 2: (inc) 6 times. (12)

Round 3: (sc, inc) 6 times. (18)

Round 4: (2 sc, inc) 6 times. (24)

Round 5: (3 sc, inc) 6 times. (30)

Round 6: (4 sc, inc) 6 times. (36)

Rounds 7–12: sc around. (36)

Round 13: (5 sc, inc) 6 times. (42)

Rounds 14–16: sc around. (42)

Insert the eyes between Rounds 12 and 13 with 7 stitches between them. Stuff the head firmly as you decrease.

Round 17: (5 sc, dec) 6 times. (36)

Round 18: (4 sc, dec) 6 times. (30)

Round 19: (3 sc, dec) 6 times. (24)

Round 20: (2 sc, dec) 6 times. (18)

Round 21: (sc, dec) 6 times. (12)

Round 22: (dec) 6 times. (6)

F/o.

Body

In light green

Round 1: mc 6. (6)

Round 2: (inc) 6 times. (12)

Round 3: (sc, inc) 6 times. (18)

Round 4: (2 sc, inc) 6 times. (24)

Round 5: (3 sc, inc) 6 times. (30)

Round 6: (4 sc, inc) 6 times. (36)

Rounds 7–9: sc around. (36)

Round 10: (4 sc, dec) 6 times. (30)

Round 11: sc around. (30)

Round 12: (3 sc, dec) 6 times. (24)

Rounds 13–15: sc around. (24)

Round 16: (2 sc, dec) 6 times. (18)

Round 17: sc around. (18)

F/o, leaving a long tail for sewing

(continued)

CHUPACABRA (CONTINUED)

Feet–Make 2

In light green

Round 1: mc 6. (6)

Round 2: (inc) 6 times. (12)

Round 3: (sc, inc) 6 times. (18)

Rounds 4–8: sc around. (18)

Round 9: (sc, dec) 6 times. (12)

Round 10: (dec) 6 times. (6)

F/o, leaving a long tail for sewing.

Front Arms–Make 2

In light green

Round 1: mc 6. (6)

Round 2: (sc, inc) 3 times. (9)

Rounds 3–14: sc around. (9)

F/o, leaving a long tail for sewing.

Ears–Make 2

In light green

Round 1: mc 4. (4)

Round 2: (sc, inc) 2 times. (6)

Round 3: (2 sc, inc) 2 times. (8)

Round 4: (3 sc, inc) 2 times. (10)

Round 5: (4 sc, inc) 2 times. (12)

Rounds 6–7: sc around. (12)

Round 8: (4 sc, dec) 2 times. (10)

Round 9: (3 sc, dec) 2 times. (8)

F/o, leaving a long tail for sewing.

Tail

In light green

Round 1: mc 6. (6)

Round 2: sc around. (6)

Round 3: (2 sc, inc) 2 times. (8)

Round 4: sc around. (8)

Round 5: (3 sc, inc) 2 times. (10)

Round 6: sc around. (10)

Round 7: (4 sc, inc) 2 times. (12)

Round 8: sc around. (12)

Round 9: (5 sc, inc) 2 times. (14)

Round 10: sc around. (14)

Round 11: (6 sc, inc) 2 times. (16)

Round 12: sc around. (16)

Round 13: (7 sc, inc) 2 times. (18)

Round 14: sc around. (18)

F/o, leaving a long tail for sewing.

Claws–Make 6

In white

Ch 3 and turn, slpst in the second chain from hook, sc in the last chain.

F/o, leaving a long tail for sewing.

Fangs–Make 2

In white

Ch 4 and turn, slpst in the second chain from hook, sc in each of the last 2 chains.

F/o, leaving a long tail for sewing.

Spikes–Make 4

In white

Ch 5 and turn, slpst in the second chain from hook, sc in the next chain, HDC in the next chain, and DC in the last chain.

F/o, leaving a long tail for sewing.

Assembly

First, whipstitch the head closed. Stuff the body firmly, and sew it to the bottom of the head. Stuff the feet and whipstitch the bottoms of them closed. Now, pin the feet and arms to the body of your Chupacabra, checking to make sure your doll remains balanced while sitting. When you are happy with the placement, sew on the limbs (no need to stuff the arms). Stuff the tail and attach it to the back of your plush. Sew the ears to either side of the head and the fangs to the front of the face, in between the eyes. Sew 3 claws to the tops of each foot, and sew the spikes down the back of the head. I attached 3 spikes, evenly spaced starting at the top of the head and going back, and 1 spike to the middle of the back of the body. Use the scissors to cut any leftover yarn tails from the limbs you've attached. Your Chupacabra is now finished!

JACKALOPE

Arguably the cutest cryptid out there, Jackalopes make their home in the grasslands of North America. They are essentially a jackrabbit with antlers, but they are much faster and smarter and more agile than your average bunny! Hunters beware—Jackalopes can fight back with their antlers. This Jackalope pattern is absolutely precious; I hope you enjoy making it as much as I did!

Materials Needed
- 4.0mm crochet hook (G hook)
- 1 (7-oz [198-g]) skein of medium worsted yarn in white (I used Red Heart's Super Saver White)
- 1 (7-oz [198-g]) skein of medium worsted yarn in brown (I used Big Twist's Value Chocolate)
- 1 pair of 12mm safety eyes
- Fiberfill, for stuffing
- Tapestry needle
- Pins, to hold the limbs in place as you sew
- Scissors
- 10-inch (25-cm) strand of pink yarn, for embroidering the nose

Abbreviations
dec—invisible decrease
F/o—fasten off
inc—increase or 2 single crochets in the same stitch
mc—magic circle
sc—single crochet

Head

In white

Round 1: mc 6. (6)

Round 2: (inc) 6 times. (12)

Round 3: (sc, inc) 6 times. (18)

Round 4: (2 sc, inc) 6 times. (24)

Round 5: (3 sc, inc) 6 times. (30)

Round 6: (4 sc, inc) 6 times. (36)

Rounds 7–12: sc around. (36)

Round 13: (5 sc, inc) 6 times. (42)

Rounds 14–16: sc around. (42)

Insert the eyes between Rounds 12 and 13 with 7 stitches between them. Stuff the head firmly as you decrease.

Round 17: (5 sc, dec) 6 times. (36)

Round 18: (4 sc, dec) 6 times. (30)

Round 19: (3 sc, dec) 6 times. (24)

Round 20: (2 sc, dec) 6 times. (18)

Round 21: (sc, dec) 6 times. (12)

Round 22: (dec) 6 times. (6)

F/o.

Body

In white

Round 1: mc 6. (6)

Round 2: (inc) 6 times. (12)

Round 3: (sc, inc) 6 times. (18)

Round 4: (2 sc, inc) 6 times. (24)

Round 5: (3 sc, inc) 6 times. (30)

Round 6: (4 sc, inc) 6 times. (36)

Rounds 7–9: sc around. (36)

Round 10: (4 sc, dec) 6 times. (30)

Round 11: sc around. (30)

Round 12: (3 sc, dec) 6 times. (24)

Rounds 13–15: sc around. (24)

Round 16: (2 sc, dec) 6 times. (18)

Round 17: sc around. (18)

F/o, leaving a long tail for sewing.

(continued)

JACKALOPE (CONTINUED)

Haunches—Make 2

In white

Round 1: mc 6. (6)

Round 2: (inc) 6 times. (12)

Round 3: (3 sc, inc) 3 times. (15)

Round 4: sc around. (15)

F/o, leaving a long tail for sewing.

Back Paws—Make 2

In white

Round 1: mc 6. (6)

Round 2: (2 sc, inc) 2 times. (8)

Round 3: sc around. (8)

F/o, leaving a long tail for sewing.

Arms—Make 2

In white

Round 1: mc 6. (6)

Round 2: (2 sc, inc) 2 times. (8)

Rounds 3–5: sc around. (8)

F/o, leaving a long tail for sewing.

Ears—Make 2

In white

Round 1: mc 4. (4)

Round 2: (sc, inc) 2 times. (6)

Round 3: (2 sc, inc) 2 times. (8)

Round 4: (3 sc, inc) 2 times. (10)

Round 5: (4 sc, inc) 2 times. (12)

Round 6: sc around. (12)

Round 7: (3 sc, inc) 3 times. (15)

Rounds 8–13: sc around. (15)

Round 14: (3 sc, dec) 3 times. (12)

Round 15: sc around. (12)

Round 16: (4 sc, dec) 2 times. (10)

F/o, leaving a long tail for sewing.

Tail

In white

Round 1: mc 6. (6)

Round 2: (2 sc, inc) 2 times. (8)

Round 3: sc around. (8)

Round 4: (dec) 4 times. (4)

F/o, leaving a long tail for sewing.

Large Antler—Make 2

In brown

Round 1: mc 6. (6)

Rounds 2–12: sc around. (6)

F/o, leaving a long tail for sewing.

Small Antler—Make 2

In brown

Round 1: mc 6. (6)

Rounds 2–5: sc around. (6)

F/o, leaving a long tail for sewing.

Assembly

Whipstitch the head closed, then stuff the body firmly and attach it to the bottom of the head. Start sewing the haunches to either side of the body, but before completely attaching them, stuff them to your desired firmness. Once you are happy, finish them off! Next, attach the back paws (stuffed) to the front of the haunches, checking the balance of your doll as you sew them to make sure they are helping keep your Jackalope upright. Next, attach the arms to either side of the body, right under where the head and body are attached (no need to stuff them).

Attach the ears to the top of the head, and attach the large antler pieces in between them. (I did not stuff mine.) Next, attach the smaller antler pieces to each of the large antlers. Attach the tail to the back of your doll; it can be used as the final step to make sure your plush remains balanced. I did not stuff my tail, but if you want to give yours a little more "fluff," it will help make it a nice, round shape! Use the scissors to cut any leftover yarn tails from the limbs you've attached. Lastly, use a scrap piece of pink yarn to embroider a little nose in between the eyes, and with that your Jackalope is done!

SANDWORM

Sandworms have grown increasingly popular over the last 50 years, appearing in many books, movies and games. They are very large wormlike creatures with a lot of teeth! They burrow underground and hunt everything using rhythmic vibrations. To escape one's notice, you must walk without allowing vibrations on the ground. I hope we never find ourselves in that situation! Luckily, this Sandworm is very tiny, and I don't think it could hurt us if it tried . . . its teeth are made out of felt!

Materials Needed

- 4.0mm crochet hook (G hook)
- 1 (7-oz [198-g]) skein of medium worsted yarn in black (I used Red Heart's Super Saver Black)
- 1 (7-oz [198-g]) skein of medium worsted yarn in light taupe (I used a Big Twist discontinued yarn, but Caron's One Pound™ Lace would be very similar)
- Fiberfill, for stuffing
- Tapestry needle
- Pins, to hold the limbs in place as you sew
- Scissors
- 1 sheet of white felt
- Fabri-Tac™ glue or hot glue

Abbreviations

F/o–fasten off

inc–increase or 2 single crochets in the same stitch

mc–magic circle

sc–single crochet

Mouth Piece

In black

Round 1: mc 6. (6)

Round 2: (inc) 6 times. (12)

Round 3: (sc, inc) 6 times. (18)

Round 4: (2 sc, inc) 6 times. (24)

Round 5: (3 sc, inc) 6 times. (30)

Round 6: (4 sc, inc) 6 times. (36)

F/o.

Body

Starts at tip of tail

In light taupe

Round 1: mc 4. (4)

Round 2: (sc, inc) 2 times. (6)

Round 3: sc around. (6)

Round 4: (2 sc, inc) 2 times. (8)

Round 5: sc around. (8)

Round 6: (3 sc, inc) 2 times. (10)

Round 7: sc around. (10)

Round 8: (4 sc, inc) 2 times. (12)

Round 9: sc around. (12)

Round 10: (3 sc, inc) 3 times. (15)

Round 11: sc around. (15)

Round 12: (4 sc, inc) 3 times. (18)

Round 13: sc around. (18)

(continued)

SANDWORM (CONTINUED)

Round 14: (5 sc, inc) 3 times. (21)

Round 15: sc around. (21)

Round 16: (6 sc, inc) 3 times. (24)

Round 17: sc around. (24)

Round 18: (3 sc, inc) 6 times. (30)

Rounds 19–20: sc around. (30)

Round 21: (4 sc, inc) 6 times. (36)

Rounds 22–31: sc around. (36)

The next step is attaching the mouth piece to the opening of the body, so pause here and make sure your Sandworm is stuffed to your desired firmness.

Round 32: sc around, inserting hook in both loops of the body *and* the mouth piece. (36)

Round 33: sc around. (36)

F/o and weave in tail.

Use the scissors to cut any leftover yarn tails.

Teeth

The finishing touch! Use the scissors to cut a bunch of tiny triangles out of the white felt and attach them around the circumference of the inner mouth using glue, pointing inward. It took me 15 teeth to get the "fullness" I was looking for, and they came out to be about ½ inch (1.3 cm) long, but you can have as many teeth as you'd like—however big or small as you see fit! Once the glue has dried, your Sandworm is finished!

Chapter 2

MAN-EATERS

In every epic tale, there is a monster—something that preys on mankind and eventually gets slain by the hero of the story. I've always had a soft spot for those monsters and often find them cute . . . even if they're supposed to be super grotesque! The story of how they came to be the way they are is also usually the one I find most intriguing. In this chapter, I have seven notorious Man-Eaters for you! You will find quite a few familiar ones among this collection: Nosferatu with his fangs (page 46), Cyclops with his giant eye (page 52) and even an adorable Werewolf with tattered shorts (page 37). My personal mission was to create all of these in such a way that you might feel how I do about them!

WEREWOLF

Man by day, a wolf-y monster by moonlight! The Werewolf is one of my favorite creatures, no matter how they are described! Of course, I am a sucker for those teenage werewolf stories. As if high school isn't hard enough, add that monthly transformation to your schedule, and you'd have intense mood swings, too! I hope you enjoy my modern take on a classic monster. We use an awesome technique in this pattern where we brush out the yarn to make it "fuzzy," which gives it such a unique texture!

Materials Needed

- 4.0mm crochet hook (G hook)
- 1 (7-oz [198-g]) skein of medium worsted yarn in brown (I used Crafter's Secret™ Big Idea Brown)
- 1 (7-oz [198-g]) skein of medium worsted yarn in grey (I used Caron's One Pound Soft Grey Mix)
- 1 pair of 9mm safety eyes
- Fiberfill, for stuffing
- Tapestry needle
- Pins, to hold the limbs in place as you sew
- Scissors
- Wire-bristled pet brush, for brushing out your Werewolf (This brush should be clean and *only* used for crafting.)
- A strand of black yarn; you won't need more than 2 feet (60 cm)

Abbreviations

dec–invisible decrease

F/o–fasten off

inc–increase or 2 single crochets in the same stitch

mc–magic circle

sc–single crochet

Head

In brown

Round 1: mc 6. (6)

Round 2: (inc) 6 times. (12)

Round 3: (sc, inc) 6 times. (18)

Round 4: (2 sc, inc) 6 times. (24)

Round 5: (3 sc, inc) 6 times. (30)

Rounds 6–11: sc around. (30)

Round 12: (4 sc, inc) 6 times. (36)

Rounds 13–16: sc around. (36)

Round 17: (4 sc, dec) 6 times. (30)

Round 18: (3 sc, dec) 6 times. (24)

Round 19: (2 sc, dec) 6 times. (18)

At this point we will stop crocheting and begin brushing out the head. Get your wire-bristled pet brush, and begin brushing your stitches. If you have never done this before, **take it slow and start gentle!** The more confident you get that you are not actually ripping the stitches, the more you can increase the speed and strength of brushing. It takes a lot of effort, so you will need to do this for quite a while to get the desired end result. (For reference, it took me about an hour to brush out my head.) It's worth it, though! It adds such a cool effect to the plushies. Also, we are doing this before placing the eyes on purpose; we don't want to scratch the safety eyes in our brushing efforts!

Place the eyes between Rounds 9 and 10 with about 6 stitches in between them. It will be hard to see the stitches now that they are all brushed out, but if you move around the "fur," you should be able to find your way. I also use a hook to help me count: I drag it across the surface and every time it dips a little, that's a stitch or a round, depending on the direction.

(continued)

WEREWOLF (CONTINUED)

Begin stuffing the head as you continue to decrease; there is no need to brush out the last 2 rows, as they will be hidden when you attach to the body.

Round 20: (sc, dec) 6 times. (12)

Round 21: (dec) 6 times. (6)

F/o.

Muzzle

In brown

Round 1: mc 6. (6)

Round 2: (inc) 6 times. (12)

Round 3: sc around. (12)

Round 4: (3 sc, inc) 3 times. (15)

Rounds 5–6: sc around. (15)

F/o, leaving a long tail for sewing, and brush out the muzzle as you did with the head.

Body

Starting with the first leg, in brown

Round 1: mc 6. (6)

Round 2: (inc) 6 times. (12)

Rounds 3–5: sc around. (12)

Change to grey

Rounds 6–7: sc around. (12)

F/o.

Second leg, in brown

Round 1: mc 6. (6)

Round 2: (inc) 6 times. (12)

Rounds 3–5: sc around. (12)

Change to grey

Rounds 6–7: sc around. (12)

Do not fasten off; join next stitch into the first leg and consider this the first stitch of Round 8.

Round 8: sc around. (24)

Rounds 9–10: sc around. (24)

Change to brown

Rounds 11–15: sc around. (24)

Round 16: (2 sc, dec) 6 times. (18)

Round 17: sc around. (18)

Round 18: (sc, dec) 6 times. (12)

F/o, leaving a long tail for sewing.

Stuff the body firmly. Brush out the brown yarn very carefully. Be cautious not to snag the grey shorts!

Tail

In brown

Round 1: mc 6. (6)

Round 2: inc, 5 sc. (7)

Round 3: inc, 6 sc. (8)

Round 4: inc, 7 sc. (9)

Rounds 5–8: sc around. (9)

F/o, leaving a long tail for sewing.

Lightly stuff the tail and brush out your stitches.

Arms—Make 2

In brown

Round 1: mc 6. (6)

Round 2: (sc, inc) 3 times. (9)

Rounds 3–9: sc around. (9)

F/o, leaving a long tail for sewing.

Brush out the arms. You're a pro by now!

Ears—Make 2

In brown

Round 1: mc 6. (6)

Round 2: sc around. (6)

Round 3: (2 sc, inc) 2 times. (8)

Round 4: sc around. (8)

Round 5: (3 sc, inc) 2 times. (10)

Round 6: sc around. (10)

Round 7: (4 sc, inc) 2 times. (12)

Round 8: (5 sc, inc) 2 times. (14)

F/o, leaving a long tail for sewing.

For the last time, brush out the ears!

Assembly

First, whipstitch the head closed. Next, make sure the body is stuffed firmly and attach it to the head. Stuff the muzzle and pin it to the middle of the head, right below the eyes. Attach it once you are happy with its positioning. Embroider the nose at the tip of the muzzle, and use the same strand to also embroider eyebrows. (This is totally optional; I felt my Werewolf needed a "concerned" expression, but you can give yours a scowl by simply changing the angle of the brows!)

Attach the arms to either side of the body (I did not stuff them) and the ears to the top of the head on either side of the starting magic circle. Pin the tail to the back of the shorts right in the middle, so it looks like it's poking through the back, and then sew it on. Use the scissors to cut any leftover yarn tails from the limbs you've attached. If you need to touch up any of his fur, you can gently brush small sections out, but be careful not to snag anything (such as the yarn you used to embroider the nose and eyebrows or the shorts). If any of the fur is too long, you can trim it with scissors, but be very careful—once you go too short, nothing can be done! Just trim little by little until you are happy with the length.

Finally, I wanted my Werewolf to appear to have tattered shorts. To achieve this look, I cut a strand of the brown yarn we used for the fur about 8 inches (20 cm) long. I embroidered a couple stripes on the shorts and then *very* gently brushed them out. This makes it look like the fur is "poking through" holes! With that, your Werewolf is done!

ZOMBIE

Brainssss! Another awesome monster, the story of Zombies has been told in so many ways to entertain us. Any time a new Zombie movie, game or show comes out, it seems everyone eats it up . . . no pun intended! You could go so many different ways with a Zombie crochet pattern. I have provided a base to go off of, but you can get as creative as you'd like! Adding tufts of hair, changing the outfit, cutting off limbs, etc. Have fun with this one; I can't wait to see what you come up with!

Head

In light green

Round 1: mc 6. (6)

Round 2: (inc) 6 times. (12)

Round 3: (sc, inc) 6 times. (18)

Round 4: (2 sc, inc) 6 times. (24)

Round 5: (3 sc, inc) 6 times. (30)

Round 6: (4 sc, inc) 6 times. (36)

Rounds 7–15: sc around. (36)

Round 16: (4 sc, dec) 6 times. (30)

Round 17: (3 sc, dec) 6 times. (24)

Partially insert the eyes between Rounds 11 and 12 with 6 stitches in between. Apply the black eye shadow around the posts of the eyes. When you are happy with how dark and how large of circles you have, secure the eyes. Stuff the head firmly as you continue to decrease.

Round 18: (2 sc, dec) 6 times. (18)

Round 19: (sc, dec) 6 times. (12)

Round 20: (dec) 6 times. (6)

F/o.

Ears–Make 2

In light green

Round 1: mc 5. (5)

Smoosh all stitches to one side of the magic circle to create a semi-circle.

F/o, leaving a long tail for sewing.

Arms–Make 2

In light green

Round 1: mc 6. (6)

Round 2: (sc, inc) 3 times. (9)

Round 3: sc around. (9)

Change to white

Rounds 4–10: sc around. (9)

F/o, leaving a long tail for sewing.

(continued)

Materials Needed

- 4.0mm crochet hook (G hook)
- 1 (7-oz [198-g]) skein of medium worsted yarn in light green (I used Red Heart's Super Saver Frosty Green)
- 1 (7-oz [198-g]) skein of medium worsted yarn in white (I used Big Twist's Value White)
- 1 (7-oz [198-g]) skein of medium worsted yarn in black (I used Big Twist's Value Black)
- 1 (7-oz [198-g]) skein of medium worsted yarn in brown (I used Crafter's Secret's Big Idea Brown)
- 1 pair of 9mm safety eyes
- Fiberfill, for stuffing
- Tapestry needle
- Pins
- Scissors
- Black eye shadow
- 1 sheet of brown felt
- Fabri-Tac glue or hot glue
- 8-inch (20-cm) strand of pink yarn, for embroidering the brain

Abbreviations

ch–chain

dec–invisible decrease

F/o–fasten off

HDC–half double crochet

inc–increase or 2 single crochets in the same stitch

mc–magic circle

sc–single crochet

ZOMBIE (CONTINUED)

Body

Starting with the first leg, in black

Round 1: mc 6. (6)

Round 2: (inc) 6 times. (12)

Round 3: sc around. (12)

Change to brown

Rounds 4–7: sc around. (12)

F/o.

Second leg, in black

Round 1: mc 6. (6)

Round 2: (inc) 6 times. (12)

Round 3: sc around. (12)

Change to brown

Rounds 4–7: sc around. (12)

Do not fasten off; join the next stitch into the first leg, and consider this the first stitch of Round 8.

Rounds 8–10: sc around. (24)

Change to white

Rounds 11–15: sc around. (24)

Round 16: (2 sc, dec) 6 times. (18)

Round 17: sc around. (18)

Round 18: (sc, dec) 6 times. (12)

F/o, leaving a long tail for sewing.

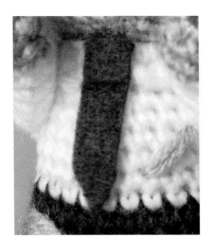

Collar–Make 2

In white

Round 1: ch 3 and turn, sc in the second chain from hook, HDC in the last chain.

F/o, leaving a long tail for sewing.

Assembly

First, whipstitch the head closed, then stuff the body firmly and sew the body to the head. Next, pin the ears to the side of the head and sew them on.
Attach the collar right in the center of the body, where the head and the body connect. Pin the arms to the side of the body and attach. I wanted mine to be "outstretched" in the classic *Brainsssss*

pose, but if you want yours to just be at his side, that is totally fine! Use the scissors to cut any leftover yarn tails from the limbs you've attached.

To make the tie, start by cutting a very skinny rectangle about 1½ x ½ inch (4 x 1.3 cm), then cut the corners off the "bottom" of the tie, making the end pointed and triangle shaped. Next, I cut a little square to be the "knot" of the tie approximately ½ x ½ inch (1.3 x 1.3 cm). I then glue the long tie portion to the middle of the collar, and when it is secured, I glue the square knot right at the top.

The final details! Cut an 8-inch (20-cm) strand of light green yarn and start embroidering "flesh" poking through his clothes to make them appear tattered. Next, use your strand of pink yarn and embroider some brain exposure on the top of his head. Once you're happy with how much brain is showing, your Zombie is finished!

SLENDER MAN

Slender Man may be one of the scariest monsters out there, and he is actually one of the newest! He was created for a Photoshop contest in 2009, and since then he has inspired many tales of horror and alleged sightings. He is a faceless, thin man wearing a black suit and has tentacles curling around behind him. He lives deep in the woods and comes out to kidnap children! Over the years, Slender Man has increased in popularity and inspired multiple movies and video games. He is really popular among children, and now you can crochet your own chibi version of him! Don't have safety eyes at the moment? Then this pattern is perfect for you, because he doesn't have any eyes!

Materials Needed

- 4.0mm crochet hook (G hook)
- 1 (7-oz [198-g]) skein of medium worsted yarn in white (I used Big Twist's Value White)
- 1 (7-oz [198-g]) skein of medium worsted yarn in black (I used Big Twist's Value Black)
- Fiberfill, for stuffing
- Tapestry needle
- Pins, to hold the limbs in place as you sew
- Scissors
- 1 sheet of red felt
- Fabri-Tac glue or hot glue

Abbreviations

ch–chain
dec–invisible decrease
F/o–fasten off
HDC–half double crochet
inc–increase or 2 single crochets in the same stitch
mc–magic circle
sc–single crochet

Head

In white

Round 1: mc 6. (6)

Round 2: (inc) 6 times. (12)

Round 3: (sc, inc) 6 times. (18)

Round 4: (2 sc, inc) 6 times. (24)

Round 5: (3 sc, inc) 6 times. (30)

Round 6: (4 sc, inc) 6 times. (36)

Rounds 7–15: sc around. (36)

Begin stuffing the head as you decrease.

Round 16: (4 sc, dec) 6 times. (30)

Round 17: (3 sc, dec) 6 times. (24)

Round 18: (2 sc, dec) 6 times. (18)

Round 19: (sc, dec) 6 times. (12)

Round 20: (dec) 6 times. (6)

F/o.

Body

Starting with the first leg, in black

Round 1: mc 6. (6)

Round 2: (inc) 6 times. (12)

Rounds 3-7: sc around. (12)

F/o.

Second leg, in black

Round 1: mc 6. (6)

Round 2: (inc) 6 times. (12)

Rounds 3-7: sc around. (12)

Do not fasten off; join the next stitch into the first leg, and consider this the first stitch of Round 8.

Round 8: sc around. (24)

Rounds 9-15: sc around. (24)

Round 16: (2 sc, dec) 6 times. (18)

Round 17: sc around. (18)

Round 18: (sc, dec) 6 times. (12)

F/o, leaving a long tail for sewing.

(continued)

SLENDER MAN (CONTINUED)

Arms—Make 2

In white

Round 1: mc 6. (6)

Round 2: (sc, inc) 3 times. (9)

Round 3: sc around. (9)

Change to black

Rounds 4–9: sc around. (9)

F/o, leaving a long tail for sewing.

Tentacles—Make 6

In black

Row 1: ch 14, turn and sc back to the beginning of the chain. (13)

F/o, leaving a long tail for sewing.

Collar—Make 2

In white

Row 1: ch 3, turn, HDC in the second chain from hook, sc in the next chain.

F/o, leaving a long tail for sewing.

Assembly

First, whipstitch the head closed. Next, stuff the body firmly and attach it to the bottom of the head. Pin the arms on either side of the torso; make sure the tops of the arms align with where the head and the body are sewn together, and sew them on (no need to stuff them). Then, pin the tentacles to the back of the doll (3 on each side), evenly spaced. When you are happy with their positioning, sew them on. Pin the collars to the front of the body, right under the head and in between the arms, and sew them on. Use the scissors to cut any leftover yarn tails from the limbs you've attached.

Lastly, cut a tie out of red felt. To make the tie, start by cutting a very skinny rectangle about 1½ x ½ inch (4 x 1.3 cm), then cut the corners off the "bottom" of the tie, making the end pointed and triangle shaped. Next, cut a little square to be the "knot" of the tie, about ½ x ½ inch (1.3 x 1.3 cm). Glue the long tie portion to the middle of the collar. When it is secured, glue the square knot right at the top. With this final detail, Slender Man is done!

NOSFERATU

Vampires are arguably one of the most popular monsters ever, and we have such a wide range of them! The lore ranges from the classic Dracula to terrifying battles for humanity. Of course, we can't forget our modern-day teenage heartthrobs! The story of the vampire has been retold in so many ways over the years, and each one has such a great new take on the classic concept. I chose to go with a classic version from the German vampire film *Nosferatu.* I hope you enjoy this vampire rendition and find these fangs as adorable as I do!

Head

In off-white

Round 1: mc 6. (6)

Round 2: (inc) 6 times. (12)

Round 3: (sc, inc) 6 times. (18)

Round 4: (2 sc, inc) 6 times. (24)

Round 5: (3 sc, inc) 6 times. (30)

Round 6: (4 sc, inc) 6 times. (36)

Rounds 7–15: sc around. (36)

Round 16: (4 sc, dec) 6 times. (30)

Round 17: (3 sc, dec) 6 times. (24)

Partially insert the eyes between Rounds 11 and 12 with 6 stitches in between. Apply the black eye shadow around the posts of the eyes. When you are happy with how dark and how large of circles you have, secure the eyes. Stuff the head firmly as you continue to decrease.

Round 18: (2 sc, dec) 6 times. (18)

Round 19: (sc, dec) 6 times. (12)

Round 20: (dec) 6 times. (6)

F/o.

Body

Starting with the first leg, in black

Round 1: mc 6. (6)

Round 2: (inc) 6 times. (12)

Rounds 3–7: sc around. (12)

F/o.

Second leg

Round 1: mc 6. (6)

Round 2: (inc) 6 times. (12)

Rounds 3–7: sc around. (12)

Do not fasten off; join the next stitch into the first leg, and consider this the first stitch of Round 8.

Round 8: sc around. (24)

Rounds 9–15: sc around. (24)

Round 16: (2 sc, dec) 6 times. (18)

Round 17: sc around. (18)

Round 18: (sc, dec) 6 times. (12)

F/o, leaving a long tail for sewing.

(continued)

Materials Needed

- 4.0mm crochet hook (G hook)
- 2.75mm crochet hook (C hook)
- 1 (7-oz [198-g]) skein of medium worsted yarn in off-white (I used I Love This Yarn's Linen)
- 1 (7-oz [198-g]) skein of medium worsted yarn in black (I used Big Twist's Value Black)
- 1 pair of 9mm safety eyes
- Fiberfill, for stuffing
- Tapestry needle
- Pins, to hold the limbs in place as you sew
- Scissors
- Black eye shadow
- 10-inch (25-cm) strand white yarn, for embroidering the fangs and robe details

Note: You will use your G hook until you get to the gown; that is done with your C hook.

Abbreviations

dec–invisible decrease

F/o–fasten off

inc–increase or 2 single crochets in the same stitch

mc–magic circle

sc–single crochet

NOSFERATU (CONTINUED)

Arms—Make 2

In off-white

Round 1: mc 4. (4)

Round 2: (sc, inc) 2 times. (6)

Round 3: sc around. (6)

Round 4: (sc, inc) 3 times. (9)

Change to black

Rounds 5–9: sc around. (9)

F/o, leaving a long tail for sewing.

Ears—Make 2

In off-white

Round 1: mc 4. (4)

Round 2: (sc, inc) 2 times. (6)

Round 3: (2 sc, inc) 2 times. (8)

Rounds 4–7: sc around. (8)

F/o, leaving a long tail for sewing.

First, whipstitch the head closed, then stuff the body firmly, pin it and sew it to the bottom of the head.

Gown

Now we will be crocheting the length of the gown.

In black

Round 1: Flip your doll around so the back is facing you, then turn it upside down (so the feet are now at the top). Insert your C hook in the middle of the back between Rounds 10 and 11, yarn over with the new black yarn, then pull it through the stitch, tightening down. You are going to continue to crochet around the body with single crochet stitches. Since we crochet in the round when we make our dolls, there is a natural spiral to the stitches. This means you will not end up connecting back to the original stitch, but you will either connect above or below it, depending on how you're looking at it. Since this is the case, you will need to "jump" a round to get back in line with where you started. I recommend doing this jump only right before you get to the final stitch and in the back of the doll. This will appear a little off if you look super closely, which is why I like to hide it on the doll's back. You should have about 24 stitches when you get back to where you started.

Rounds 2–9: sc around. (~24)

F/o and weave in tail.

Assembly

Next, attach the arms to either side of the body (no need to stuff them). Attach the ears to the sides of his head. Use the scissors to cut any leftover yarn tails. Use the white yarn to embroider fangs and gown embellishments. Now your Nosferatu is ready to lurk about an abandoned castle!

MINOTAUR

The Minotaur is a creature I will always pity. In Greek mythology, he is often depicted as a grotesque monster that is a mix of a man and a bull. His job is to guard a labyrinth, and the only human contact he has is when he is hunting them, as they are his food—and a Minotaur has to do what a Minotaur has to do! Perhaps you can change your Minotaur's ways. I love adding non-yarn details to my dolls, and this Minotaur has some awesome ones you can try! We use crafting wire for his nose ring and felt for his loincloth. All these different textures give him such a unique and "complete" look. You'll see what I mean!

Head

In medium brown

Round 1: mc 6. (6)

Round 2: (inc) 6 times. (12)

Round 3: (sc, inc) 6 times. (18)

Round 4: (2 sc, inc) 6 times. (24)

Round 5: (3 sc, inc) 6 times. (30)

Round 6: (4 sc, inc) 6 times. (36)

Rounds 7–12: sc around. (36)

Round 13: (5 sc, inc) 6 times. (42)

Rounds 14–16: sc around. (42)

Insert the eyes between Rounds 12 and 13 with 7 stitches between them. Stuff the head firmly as you decrease.

Round 17: (5 sc, dec) 6 times. (36)

Round 18: (4 sc, dec) 6 times. (30)

Round 19: (3 sc, dec) 6 times. (24)

Round 20: (2 sc, dec) 6 times. (18)

Round 21: (sc, dec) 6 times. (12)

Round 22: (dec) 6 times. (6)

F/o.

Body

Starting with the first leg, in dark brown

Round 1: mc 6. (6)

Round 2: (inc) 6 times. (12)

Round 3: (sc, inc) 6 times. (18)

Round 4: BLO sc around. (18)

Round 5: sc around. (18)

Change to medium brown

Rounds 6–9: sc around. (18)

F/o.

Second leg, in dark brown

Round 1: mc 6. (6)

Round 2: (inc) 6 times. (12)

Round 3: (sc, inc) 6 times. (18)

Round 4: BLO sc around. (18)

Round 5: sc around. (18)

(continued)

Materials Needed

- 4.0mm crochet hook (G hook)
- 1 (7-oz [198-g]) skein of medium worsted yarn in brown (I used Red Heart's Super Saver Café Latte)
- 1 (7-oz [198-g]) skein of medium worsted yarn in dark brown (I used Crafter's Secret's Big Idea Brown)
- 1 (7-oz [198-g]) skein of medium worsted yarn in off-white (I used I Love This Yarn's Linen)
- 1 (7-oz [198-g]) skein of medium worsted yarn in grey (I used Caron's One Pound Soft Grey Mix)
- 1 pair of 12mm safety eyes
- Fiberfill, for stuffing
- 8 inches (20 cm) gold aluminum crafting wire
- 2 sheets of felt in two different shades of brown
- Tapestry needle, pins and scissors
- Fabri-Tac glue or hot glue

Abbreviations

BLO—crochet only in the back loop of the stitch for the following round

ch—chain

dec—invisible decrease

F/o—fasten off

inc—increase or 2 single crochets in the same stitch

mc—magic circle

sc—single crochet

MINOTAUR (CONTINUED)

Change to medium brown

Rounds 6–9: sc around. (18)

Do not fasten off; join the next stitch into the first leg, and consider this the first stitch of Round 10.

Rounds 10–11: sc around. (36)

Round 12: (4 sc, dec) 6 times. (30)

Rounds 13–16: sc around. (30)

Round 17: (3 sc, dec) 6 times. (24)

Rounds 18–20: sc around. (24)

Round 21: (2 sc, dec) 6 times. (18)

Round 22: sc around. (18)

F/o, leaving a long tail for sewing.

Muzzle

In medium brown

Round 1: ch 7, turn and sc around the entire foundation chain, putting 2 stitches in each end of the chain. (12)

Round 2: (sc, inc) 6 times. (18)

Rounds 3–4: sc around. (18)

F/o, leaving a long tail for sewing.

Before moving on from the muzzle, we are going to place the nose ring. Fold the crafting wire in half, keeping the "loop" rounded. Insert the two wire ends into the muzzle, and twist them together to secure. Make sure the "loop" that is outside of the muzzle still has plenty of space so it looks like a ring that is hanging. Trim the excess wire inside the muzzle, and be very careful when stuffing later, as you don't want the ring to get twisted or deformed when you're shoving fluff in there! If you do not have crafting wire, you can use golden yarn or a thin strip of felt; instead of twisting the ends to secure, you can tie them off with a knot.

Ears—Make 2

In medium brown

Round 1: mc 6. (6)

Round 2: (inc) 6 times. (12)

Round 3: (sc, inc) 6 times. (18)

Round 4: (2 sc, inc) 6 times. (24)

Fold the ear in half, turn, (no need to chain up) sc to other side. (12)

F/o, leaving a long tail for sewing.

Horns—Make 2

In off-white

Round 1: mc 6. (6)

Round 2: sc around. (6)

Round 3: (2 sc, inc) 2 times. (8)

Rounds 4–5: sc around. (8)

Round 6: (3 sc, inc) 2 times. (10)

Rounds 7–11: sc around. (10)

F/o, leaving a long tail for sewing.

Arms—Make 2

In medium brown

Round 1: mc 6. (6)

Round 2: (inc) 6 times. (12)

Round 3: sc around. (12)

Change to grey

Rounds 4–6: sc around. (12)

Change back to medium brown

Rounds 7–12: sc around. (12)

F/o, leaving a long tail for sewing.

Assembly

First, whipstitch the head closed, then stuff the body firmly and sew the body to the head. Next, very carefully pin the muzzle to the center of the head, right below the eyes, and attach it. I recommend attaching it about 75 percent of the way, then gently stuffing. We are taking extra precautions here due to the nose ring; we don't want to bend it while assembling the doll! Once it is firm enough, finish sewing the rest of the way.

Next we are going to make the loincloth. Cut 2 trapezoids in the lighter shade of brown felt, and glue 1 to the front of the doll and the other to the back. Next, cut a long, skinny strip of the dark brown felt and glue it over the very top of the felt you just glued on. This piece will wrap around the waist and will overlap slightly.

Next, stuff the arms lightly and attach 1 to each side of the body. Attach the ears to either side of the head, and lightly stuff and attach the horns. (We are keeping the horns less stuffed so we can manipulate them to appear more curved then they really are!) Use the scissors to cut any leftover yarn tails. With this, your Minotaur is finished!

CYCLOPS

A one-eyed giant whose diet consists of humans and who expertly wields a club? Sounds pretty scary . . . but look at that smile! It's so sweet! He has to be misunderstood . . . right?! Greek mythology was not kind to the Cyclopes throughout time. They called them ferocious, unintelligent, cave-dwelling cannibals! Maybe as you make your Cyclops doll, you will form a new opinion on them. I had a lot of fun with this design and love how he turned out; I hope you enjoy him as well!

Head

In preferred skin tone

Round 1: mc 6. (6)

Round 2: (inc) 6 times. (12)

Round 3: (sc, inc) 6 times. (18)

Round 4: (2 sc, inc) 6 times. (24)

Round 5: (3 sc, inc) 6 times. (30)

Round 6: (4 sc, inc) 6 times. (36)

Rounds 7–12: sc around. (36)

Round 13: (5 sc, inc) 6 times. (42)

Rounds 14–16: sc around. (42)

Before placing the eye, cut out an eye-shaped piece of felt and insert it behind the eye post. Insert the eye between Rounds 11 and 12. Stuff the head firmly as you decrease.

Round 17: (5 sc, dec) 6 times. (36)

Round 18: (4 sc, dec) 6 times. (30)

Round 19: (3 sc, dec) 6 times. (24)

Round 20: (2 sc, dec) 6 times. (18)

Round 21: (sc, dec) 6 times. (12)

Round 22: (dec) 6 times. (6)

F/o.

Body

Starting with the first leg, in preferred skin tone

Round 1: mc 6. (6)

Round 2: (inc) 6 times. (12)

Round 3: (sc, inc) 6 times. (18)

Rounds 4–8: sc around. (18)

F/o.

Second leg, in preferred skin tone

Round 1: mc 6. (6)

Round 2: (inc) 6 times. (12)

Round 3: (sc, inc) 6 times. (18)

Rounds 4–8: sc around. (18)

Do not fasten off; join the next stitch into the first leg, and consider this the first stitch of Round 9. Also, I recommend changing colors during the last stitch of Round 8 of the second leg, as Round 9 begins in a different color.

(continued)

Materials Needed

- 4.0mm crochet hook (G hook)
- 2.75mm crochet hook (C hook)
- 1 (7-oz [198-g]) skein of medium worsted yarn in preferred skin tone (I used Red Heart's Super Saver Buff)
- 1 (7-oz [198-g]) skein of medium worsted yarn in dark brown (I used Crafter's Secret's Big Idea Brown)
- 1 (7-oz [198-g]) skein of medium worsted yarn in medium brown (I used Red Heart's Super Saver Café Latte)
- 15mm safety eye
- Fiberfill, for stuffing
- Tapestry needle
- Pins, to hold the limbs in place as you sew
- Scissors
- 1 sheet of white felt
- Small amount of embroidery thread in black and white, less than 10 inches (25 cm) of each

Note: You will use your G hook until you get to the kilt; that is done with your C hook.

Abbreviations

dec—invisible decrease

F/o—fasten off

inc—increase or 2 single crochets in the same stitch

mc—magic circle

sc—single crochet

CYCLOPS (CONTINUED)

Change to dark brown

Rounds 9–10: sc around. (36)

Round 11: (4 sc, dec) 6 times. (30)

Round 12: sc around. (30)

Change back to preferred skin tone

Rounds 13–15: sc around. (30)

Round 16: (3 sc, dec) 6 times. (24)

Rounds 17–19: sc around. (24)

Round 20: (2 sc, dec) 6 times. (18)

Round 21: sc around. (18)

F/o, leaving a long tail for sewing.

Arms–Make 2

Round 1: mc 6. (6)

Round 2: (inc) 6 times. (12)

Round 3: (3 sc, inc) 3 times. (15)

Round 4: sc around. (15)

Round 5: (3 sc, dec) 3 times. (12)

Rounds 6–7: sc around. (12)

Round 8: (4 sc, dec) 2 times. (10)

Rounds 9–12: sc around. (10)

F/o, leaving a long tail for sewing.

Ears–Make 2

Round 1: mc 5. (5)

Smoosh all stitches to one side of the magic circle to create a semi-circle.

F/o, leaving a long tail for sewing.

Whipstitch the head closed. Next, stuff the body firmly and attach it to the head.

Club

In dark brown

Round 1: mc 6. (6)

Round 2: (inc) 6 times. (12)

Rounds 3–5: sc around. (12)

Round 6: (2 sc, dec) 3 times. (9)

Stuff the club firmly as you continue to decrease.

Rounds 7–8: sc around. (9)

Round 9: (sc, dec) 3 times. (6)

Round 10: sc around. (6)

F/o, leaving a long tail for sewing.

Kilt

Now, we are going to work on crocheting the kilt. First, you'll gather your C hook and the medium brown yarn, or whatever color you choose to make the kilt. Now, turn your Cyclops around and flip him upside down.

Insert your C hook in the middle of the back between Rounds 11 and 12, yarn over with the color you have selected, then pull it through the stitch, tightening down. You are going to continue to crochet around the body with single crochet stitches. Since we crochet in the round when we make our dolls, there is a natural spiral to the stitches. This means you will not end up connecting back to the original stitch, but either above or below it, depending on how you're looking at it. Since this is the case, you will need to "jump" a round to get back in line with where you started. I recommend doing this jump only right before you get to the final stitch and in the back of the doll. This will appear a little off if you look super closely, which is why I like to hide it on the doll's back.

Once you have jumped that stitch, you will end up back in line with where you started and finish off that round by making an sc back into the original stitch. We will call this the end of Round 1, which should have a total of 30 stitches in it. (If you have more or less, do not worry about the count; the important thing is that you have crocheted all the way around and have a nice line of stitches in which to place the following rounds).

Round 2: sc in each original stitch you laid as the foundation. (~30)

Round 3: (sc, inc) 15 times. (~45)

Again, do not worry if your stitch count is off by a few, just keep going—your kilt will look great!

Rounds 4–5: sc around. (~45)

F/o, leaving a long tail so you can weave it through the kilt and hide it within the body.

Assembly

Once you hide the tails from the kilt, lightly stuff the arms and attach them on either side of the body. Next, pin the ears on each side of the head and sew them on. Lastly, attach the club to your Cyclops's hand. The final detail is embroidering a smile (or frown if you want him to be more ferocious.); do this with black embroidery thread, then use a small amount of white yarn to embroider his little teeth in the corners of his mouth. Of course, you have complete artistic liberty to make your Cyclops however you see fit! Use the scissors to cut and weave in any leftover yarn tails.

MANTICORE

The Manticore is a man-eating beast that has lion features, a scorpion's tail and dragon's wings. They are fierce hunters that originated in Greek mythology—as I am sure you can imagine they would be, given their features. When in a pack, they are even more dangerous . . . so keep that in mind if you choose to make many at once! However, the creature Manticores fear the most is a dragon. So, if you plan on making the Dragon (page 139) as well, it should be able to keep your Manticores in line! One of my favorite parts of making this doll was the mane. It may seem tedious while you are attaching all those strands, but once it's nice and full it is so soft and fun to pet!

Materials Needed

- 4.0mm crochet hook (G hook)
- 1 (7-oz [198-g]) skein of medium worsted yarn in light yellow (I used I Love This Yarn's Buttercup)
- 1 (7-oz [198-g]) skein of medium worsted yarn in red (I used Caron's Simply Soft Autumn Red)
- 1 (7-oz [198-g]) skein of medium worsted yarn in in brown (I used Crafter's Secret's Big Idea Brown)
- 1 pair of 9mm safety eyes
- Fiberfill, for stuffing
- Tapestry needle
- Pins, to hold the limbs in place as you sew
- Scissors
- 10-inch (25-cm) strand of black yarn, for embroidering the nose

Abbreviations

ch–chain
dec–invisible decrease
F/o–fasten off
inc–increase or 2 single crochets in the same stitch
mc–magic circle
sc–single crochet

Head

In light yellow

Round 1: mc 6. (6)

Round 2: (inc) 6 times. (12)

Round 3: (sc, inc) 6 times. (18)

Round 4: (2 sc, inc) 6 times. (24)

Round 5: (3 sc, inc) 6 times. (30)

Rounds 6–10: sc around. (30)

Round 11: (4 sc, inc) 6 times. (36)

Rounds 12–15: sc around. (36)

Place the eyes between Rounds 10 and 11 with 6 stitches in between. Stuff the head firmly as you decrease.

Round 16: (4 sc, dec) 6 times. (30)

Round 17: (3 sc, dec) 6 times. (24)

Round 18: (2 sc, dec) 6 times. (18)

Round 19: (sc, dec) 6 times. (12)

Round 20: (dec) 6 times. (6)

F/o.

Muzzle

In light yellow

Round 1: mc 6. (6)

Round 2: (inc) 6 times. (12)

Round 3: (3 sc, inc) 3 times. (15)

Rounds 4–6: sc around. (15)

F/o, leaving a long tail for sewing.

(continued)

MANTICORE (CONTINUED)

Ears–Make 2

In light yellow

Round 1: mc 6. (6)

Round 2: (2 sc, inc) 2 times. (8)

Round 3: sc around. (8)

F/o, leaving a long tail for sewing.

Legs–Make 4

In light yellow

Round 1: mc 6. (6)

Round 2: (inc) 6 times. (12)

Rounds 3–9: sc around. (12)

F/o, leaving a long tail for sewing.

Horns–Make 2

In red

Round 1: mc 6. (6)

Rounds 2–4: sc around. (6)

F/o, leaving a long tail for sewing.

Body

In light yellow

Round 1: mc 6. (6)

Round 2: (inc) 6 times. (12)

Round 3: (sc, inc) 6 times. (18)

Round 4: (2 sc, inc) 6 times. (24)

Rounds 5–15: sc around. (24)

Round 16: (2 sc, dec) 6 times. (18)

F/o, leaving a long tail for sewing.

Wings–Make 2

The wings are made in rows, not rounds. Please read the pattern carefully.

In red

Row 1: ch 5, turn.

Row 2: Start in the second chain from hook, 4 sc, ch 4 and turn.

Row 3: Start in the second chain from hook, 7 sc, ch 1 and turn.

Row 4: Start in the second chain from hook, 4 sc, ch 4 and turn.

Row 5: Start in the second chain from hook, 7 sc, ch 3 and turn.

Row 6: Start in the second chain from hook, 6 sc, ch 4 and turn.

Row 7: Start in the second chain from hook, 9 sc, do not chain or turn.

Row 8: sc around the top of the wing (you will be creating evenly spaced stitches along this ridge).

F/o, leaving a long tail for sewing.

Tail: Round Segments–Make 3

In red

Round 1: mc 6. (6)

Round 2: (inc) 6 times. (12)

Round 3–5: sc around. (12)

Round 6: (dec) 6 times. (6)

F/o, leaving a long tail for sewing.

Tail: Stinger–Make 1

In red

Round 1: mc 4. (4)

Round 2: inc, 3 sc. (5)

Round 3: inc, 4 sc. (6)

Round 4: inc, 5 sc. (7)

Round 5: inc, 6 sc. (8)

F/o, leaving a long tail for sewing.

Assembly

First, whipstitch the head closed. Next stuff the muzzle, pin it and sew it onto the head, right between the eyes. Next, stuff the body and attach it to the back of the head. Our Manticore will be in a laying down position, so their tummy will be touching the ground and in line with the bottom of the head. Next, attach the ears and the horns on top of the head (no need to stuff these). I positioned my horns a little more forward on the head so the ears could be more tucked into the mane.

For the mane, we will need to cut about 100 (4-inch [10-cm]) strands of brown yarn. Start attaching them to the head using the latch hook method. Once the mane is nice and full, it is time to trim it down. Be careful when cutting the hair; once you go too short, there is no going back! If you do go too short and are unhappy with the length, just undo the strands in that section and start over. Embroider the nose using a strand of black yarn.

Next, stuff all of the legs and attach them to the body. I wanted my Manticore to lay flat in a sort of "sploot" position, so I was very careful when sewing on my legs to make sure they were flush with the bottom of the body and wouldn't be lifting it. I always recommend pinning your limbs before sewing, then checking to

make sure they are where you want them to be after every single one is attached. It is very easy for a pin to be loose and a limb to move; then while you're attaching it, you realize your doll isn't quite as symmetrical as when you began.

Pin the wings to the Manticore's back in whatever position you would like them to be in. Sew them on when you are happy with their placement.

Time for the last part—the tail! Start by stuffing all the round segments firmly; the stinger will not need to be stuffed. Pin the first round segment piece to the

back of the Manticore where you would like the tail to begin, then sew it on. For the next round segment piece, position it on the first to begin creating the curve of the tail. When you're happy with the positioning, sew it on. Repeat this step for the third and final round piece. The last step is the stinger —with the increases involved when crocheting this part, it naturally has a curve as well. Use this to your advantage when sewing it on, so it finishes the curve you began to create when sewing on the round segment pieces. Use the scissors to cut any leftover yarn tails, and your Manticore is complete!

Chapter 3

CREATURES OF THE DEEP

The ocean remains one of Earth's last "unknowns," with over 80 percent of it unexplored! Miles of deep caverns, underwater volcanoes . . . and potential portals to other worlds. In all seriousness, the oceans are fascinating even without sprinkling in lore and mythology. However, that's not what this book is about! In the following chapter, we are going to look at some adorable and beautiful water dwelling creatures from the Mermaid (page 65) to Kaiju (page 79). I'm sure there will be something in this chapter that you'll need to add to your personal collection. For me, it was the Kappa (page 75)— that little guy stole my heart!

KRAKEN

Krakens are giant cephalopods that live off the coast of Scandinavia. When I say big—I mean big! Reported sightings share they are over a mile (1.6 km) in length! They are incredibly strong and agile, and have been plaguing sailors since the beginning of time, according to legend.

I don't think crocheting a life-size Kraken would be possible in one lifetime . . . so, I have created this miniature version for us. They are so much cuter when they're smaller . . . and safer too! Be careful how much you feed it and how much space you give it to grow; we don't want things getting out of hand! This pattern is probably the quickest one in this book, and it is an excellent stash-buster, as it takes so little yarn!

Materials Needed

- 4.0mm crochet hook (G hook)
- 1 (7-oz [198-g]) skein of super bulky yarn in green (I used a Big Twist discontinued yarn, but double-stranding Big Twist's Value Varsity Green would be very similar)
- 1 pair of 9mm safety eyes
- Fiberfill, for stuffing
- Tapestry needle
- Pins, to hold the limbs in place as you sew
- Scissors

Abbreviations

ch—chain
dec—invisible decrease
F/o—fasten off
HDC—half double crochet
inc—increase or 2 single crochets in the same stitch
mc—magic circle
sc—single crochet
slpst—slip stitch

Head/Body

Round 1: mc 6. (6)

Round 2: (inc) 6 times. (12)

Round 3: (sc, inc) 6 times. (18)

Round 4: (2 sc, inc) 6 times. (24)

Rounds 5–8: sc around. (24)

Round 9: (dec) 4 times, sc in the remaining 16 stitches. (20)

Round 10: (dec) 2 times, sc in the remaining 16 stitches. (18)

Rounds 11–13: sc around. (18)

Round 14: (dec) 2 times, sc in the remaining 14 stitches. (16)

Insert the eyes between Rounds 12 and 13 with 6 stitches in between them. Place them on the "front" side of the Kraken, the "back" being where the decreases are. Stuff the head/body firmly as you continue from this point.

Tentacles—Make 8

In this next round we will be making the tentacles; take your time and read each step carefully!

Round 15: slpst into the next stitch, ([ch 16 and turn, sc in the next 10 stitches, starting from the second chain from hook, HDC in the remaining 5 stitches]. Skip the immediate next stitch from the body, and slpst into the next stitch beyond it.); repeat this process 8 times.

When you finish the last tentacle, F/o.

(continued)

KRAKEN (CONTINUED)

Closing Piece

Round 1: mc 6. (6)

Round 2: (inc) 6 times. (12)

F/o, leaving a long tail for sewing.

This piece is purposefully smaller than the opening of the head/body, so it can tuck slightly inside the Kraken.

Assembly

After ensuring that the head/body is firmly stuffed, tuck the closing piece inside the body and sew it in. Use the scissors to cut the leftover yarn tail. Help your tentacles curl by giving them a twist following their natural curling direction, and that's it! Your Kraken is done!

MERMAID

Rare sightings by sailors and shipwreck survivors tell of beautiful women who are half human, half fish. Now, depending on whom you ask, some claim mermaids have been known to lure sailors into storms and assured disaster, while others claim they save who they can from drowning. I like to believe the latter! This pattern is extremely versatile; the color combinations are endless, and you can style the hair any way you'd like.

Materials Needed

- 4.0mm crochet hook (G hook)
- 1 (7-oz [198-g]) skein of medium worsted yarn in preferred skin tone (I used I Love This Yarn's Toasted Almond)
- 1 (7-oz [198-g]) skein of medium worsted yarn in purple (I used Caron's Simply Soft Lavender Blue)
- 1 pair of 9mm safety eyes
- Fiberfill, for stuffing
- Tapestry needle
- Pins, to hold the limbs in place as you sew
- Scissors
- Fabri-Tac glue or hot glue

Abbreviations

dec—invisible decrease

F/o—fasten off

inc—increase or 2 single crochets in the same stitch

mc—magic circle

sc—single crochet

Head

In preferred skin tone

Round 1: mc 6. (6)

Round 2: (inc) 6 times. (12)

Round 3: (sc, inc) 6 times. (18)

Round 4: (2 sc, inc) 6 times. (24)

Round 5: (3 sc, inc) 6 times. (30)

Round 6: (4 sc, inc) 6 times. (36)

Rounds 7–15: sc around. (36)

Insert the eyes between Rounds 11 and 12 with 6 stitches in between. Start stuffing the head as you decrease.

Round 16: (4 sc, dec) 6 times. (30)

Round 17: (3 sc, dec) 6 times. (24)

Round 18: (2 sc, dec) 6 times. (18)

Round 19: (sc, dec) 6 times. (12)

Round 20: (dec) 6 times. (6)

F/o.

Wig Cap

In purple

Round 1: mc 6. (6)

Round 2: (inc) 6 times. (12)

Round 3: (sc, inc) 6 times. (18)

Round 4: (2 sc, inc) 6 times. (24)

Round 5: (3 sc, inc) 6 times. (30)

Round 6: (4 sc, inc) 6 times. (36)

Rounds 7–11: sc around. (36)

F/o, leaving an extra long tail for sewing.

Hair

To begin making hair similar to the doll that is pictured, first sew the wig cap to the top of the head. Leave any excess yarn from sewing attached; we will use it to attach the strands of hair. If it is not long enough (you need about 10 inches [25 cm]), then cut a new strand of yarn and use it instead. Weave the strand of yarn to the front of the wig cap; this is where we will begin attaching our hair.

(continued)

MERMAID (CONTINUED)

Next cut about 40 strands of purple yarn, about 8 inches (20 cm) long. Begin sewing bundles of them to the wig cap. I find 4 strands is a perfect thickness for each section. Keep your sewing line straight, as this will be where the hair parts. Pull your sewing strand very tight every time you secure a hair bundle, and maintain that same tightness as you continue down the wig cap. I usually stop attaching bundles of hair once I get to the back of the head (where attaching the hair would become a vertical task). The last step is to apply a very thin line of glue on each side of the part to make sure the hair doesn't easily come out of the sewn part we just created. Remember: A little bit of glue goes a very long way, so keep the line of glue very thin. We don't want it to bleed through the hair and show. Set the head aside somewhere safe until the glue has dried. Leave the hair strands long for now; trimming is the very last thing we do!

Body

In purple

Round 1: mc 6. (6)

Round 2: sc around. (6)

Round 3: (sc, inc) 3 times. (9)

Round 4: sc around. (9)

Round 5: (2 sc, inc) 3 times. (12)

Round 6: sc around. (12)

Round 7: (3 sc, inc) 3 times. (15)

Rounds 8–9: sc around. (15)

Round 10: (4 sc, inc) 3 times. (18)

Rounds 11–12: sc around. (18)

Round 13: (5 sc, inc) 3 times. (21)

Rounds 14–15: sc around. (21)

Round 16: (6 sc, inc) 3 times. (24)

Round 17: sc around. (24)

Change to preferred skin tone

Rounds 18–20: sc around. (24)

Round 21: (2 sc, dec) 6 times. (18)

Change to purple

Rounds 22–24: sc around. (18)

Change to preferred skin tone

Round 25: (sc, dec) 6 times. (12)

Round 26: sc around. (12)

F/o, leaving a long tail for sewing.

Arms—Make 2

In preferred skin tone

Round 1: mc 6. (6)

Rounds 2–11: sc around. (6)

F/o, leaving a long tail for sewing.

Tail Fin—Make 2

In purple

Round 1: mc 4. (4)

Round 2: (sc, inc) 2 times. (6)

Round 3: (2 sc, inc) 2 times. (8)

Round 4: (3 sc, inc) 2 times. (10)

Round 5: (4 sc, inc) 2 times. (12)

Rounds 6–7: sc around. (12)

Round 8: (4 sc, dec) 2 times. (10)

Round 9: (3 sc, dec) 2 times. (8)

F/o, leaving a long tail for sewing.

Assembly

Once the glue has dried, whipstitch the bottom of the head closed.

Stuff the body firmly, making sure to get stuffing to the very tip of the tail, too. Attach the body to the bottom of the head. Pin the arms to either side of the body and attach (no need to stuff them). Next, flatten the fins and attach them to the bottom of the tail (no need to stuff these). Use the scissors to cut any leftover yarn tails. Lastly, trim the hair. Take it slow—you can always cut more off, but once you go too short, there isn't much that can be done to go back! Once you are happy with your hair length, your Mermaid is done!

KELPIE

Kelpies are supernatural water horses that originated in Celtic folklore, although there are variations of the same beast in many cultures. They are shapeshifters that can transform themselves to appear as a land horse or a human, and they lure unsuspecting mortals to the water where they will have the advantage and be able to eat them! Stay clear of these predators! They are very beautiful, despite being monsters, so here is a crochet pattern to make your own. It's pretty small, so you should be able to take it if it tries to turn on you.

Materials Needed

- 4.0mm crochet hook (G hook)
- 1 (7-oz [198-g]) skein of medium worsted yarn in medium green (I used I Love This Yarn's Light Sage)
- 1 (7-oz [198-g]) skein of medium worsted yarn in dark green (I used I Love This Yarn's Forest Green)
- 1 pair of 9mm safety eyes
- Fiberfill, for stuffing
- Tapestry needle
- Pins, to hold the limbs in place as you sew
- Scissors

Abbreviations

dec–invisible decrease
F/o–fasten off
inc–increase or 2 single crochets in the same stitch
mc–magic circle
sc–single crochet

Head

In medium green

Round 1: mc 6. (6)

Round 2: (inc) 6 times. (12)

Round 3: (sc, inc) 6 times. (18)

Round 4: (2 sc, inc) 6 times. (24)

Rounds 5–8: sc around. (24)

Round 9: (3 sc, inc) 6 times. (30)

Round 10: (4 sc, inc) 6 times. (36)

Rounds 11–13: sc around. (36)

Round 14: (4 sc, dec) 6 times. (30)

Round 15: sc around. (30)

Insert the eyes between Rounds 9 and 10 with 9 stitches in between. Start stuffing the head as you decrease.

Round 16: (3 sc, dec) 6 times. (24)

Round 17: (2 sc, dec) 6 times. (18)

Round 18: (sc, dec) 6 times. (12)

Round 19: (dec) 6 times. (6)

F/o.

Ears–Make 2

In medium green

Round 1: mc 4. (4)

Round 2: (sc, inc) 2 times. (6)

Round 3: (2 sc, inc) 2 times. (8)

Round 4: (3 sc, inc) 2 times. (10)

Round 5: (4 sc, inc) 2 times. (12)

Rounds 6–7: sc around. (12)

Round 8: (dec) 6 times. (6)

F/o, leaving a long tail for sewing.

(continued)

KELPIE (CONTINUED)

Body

In medium green

Round 1: mc 6. (6)

Round 2: (inc) 6 times. (12)

Round 3: (sc, inc) 6 times. (18)

Round 4: (2 sc, inc) 6 times. (24)

Round 5: (3 sc, inc) 6 times. (30)

Rounds 6–9: sc around. (30)

Round 10: (3 sc, dec) 6 times. (24)

Rounds 11–15: sc around. (24)

Round 16: (2 sc, dec) 6 times. (18)

Round 17: (sc, dec) 6 times. (12)

F/o, leaving a long tail for sewing.

Legs–Make 2

In dark green

Round 1: mc 6. (6)

Round 2: (inc) 6 times. (12)

Round 3: (3 sc, inc) 3 times. (15)

Rounds 4–5: sc around. (15)

Round 6: (3 sc, dec) 3 times. (12)

Change to medium green

Rounds 7–9: sc around. (12)

Round 10: (2 sc, dec) 3 times. (9)

Rounds 11–15: sc around. (9)

F/o, leaving a long tail for sewing.

Tail

In medium green

Round 1: mc 6. (6)

Round 2: sc around. (6)

Round 3: (sc, inc) 3 times. (9)

Round 4: sc around. (9)

Round 5: (2 sc, inc) 3 times. (12)

Round 6: sc around. (12)

Round 7: (3 sc, inc) 3 times. (15)

Rounds 8–9: sc around. (15)

Round 10: (4 sc, inc) 3 times. (18)

Rounds 11–12: sc around. (18)

Round 13: (5 sc, inc) 3 times. (21)

Rounds 14–15: sc around. (21)

Round 16: (6 sc, inc) 3 times. (24)

Round 17: sc around. (24)

F/o, leaving a long tail for sewing.

Tail Fin–Make 2

In medium green

Round 1: mc 4. (4)

Round 2: (sc, inc) 2 times. (6)

Round 3: (2 sc, inc) 2 times. (8)

Round 4: (3 sc, inc) 2 times. (10)

Round 5: (4 sc, inc) 2 times. (12)

Rounds 6–7: sc around. (12)

Round 8: (4 sc, dec) 2 times. (10)

Round 9: (3 sc, dec) 2 times. (8)

F/o, leaving a long tail for sewing.

Assembly

Whipstitch the head closed, then stuff the body firmly and attach it to the bottom of the head. Stuff the legs and attach them to either side of the front of the body, positioning them so your Kelpie can lean on them and help itself balance; this will keep it sitting upright. Next, stuff the tail and pin it to the back of the body. I wanted mine slightly to the side so you could see the fins even when looking at it straight on. Sew the tail on when you are happy with its positioning; the tail can also help balance the plush if the front legs aren't doing the trick. Sew the tail fins to either side of the tip of the tail (no need to stuff them). Sew the ears to the top of the head (no need to stuff either). Use the scissors to cut any leftover yarn tails.

Finally, we will work on the mane. First, cut about 60 (5-inch [13-cm]) strands of the dark green yarn. Attach each strand to the head of the Kelpie using the latch hook method. I made my mane 4 strands wide and started right in front of the ears, working my way down the back of its head. Once you have your mane filled in to its desired thickness, you can trim it or leave it long. I did not trim mine; I liked the length it came out to! Once you are happy with your mane length and thickness, your Kelpie is done!

GRINDYLOW

Grindylows are little, monstrous, ravenous, water spirits from English folklore. They live in the shallows of lakes and marshes, and prey on small children who venture too close to the water's edge! I try to make even grotesque, evil things little and cute, and I hope you can appreciate my efforts with this one! Enjoy making your Grindylows, and use them as a reminder to small children to not venture into the water without adult supervision, just like the legends have been used.

Materials Needed

- 4.0mm crochet hook (G hook)
- 1 (7-oz [198-g]) skein of medium worsted yarn in soft green (I used Loops & Threads® Impeccable™ Fern)
- 1 pair of 12mm safety eyes
- Fiberfill, for stuffing
- Tapestry needle
- Pins, to hold the limbs in place as you sew
- Scissors
- 10-inch (25-cm) strand white yarn
- 10-inch (25-cm) strand black embroidery thread

Abbreviations

dec–invisible decrease
F/o–fasten off
inc–increase or 2 single crochets in the same stitch
mc–magic circle
sc–single crochet

Head

Round 1: mc 6. (6)

Round 2: (inc) 6 times. (12)

Round 3: (sc, inc) 6 times. (18)

Round 4: (2 sc, inc) 6 times. (24)

Round 5: (3 sc, inc) 6 times. (30)

Round 6: (4 sc, inc) 6 times. (36)

Rounds 7–11: sc around. (36)

Round 12: (5 sc, inc) 6 times. (42)

Rounds 13–15: sc around. (42)

Insert the eyes between Rounds 12 and 13 with 7 stitches in between them. Stuff the head firmly as you decrease.

Round 16: (5 sc, dec) 6 times. (36)

Round 17: (4 sc, dec) 6 times. (30)

Round 18: (3 sc, dec) 6 times. (24)

Round 19: (2 sc, dec) 6 times. (18)

Round 20: (sc, dec) 6 times. (12)

Round 21: (dec) 6 times. (6)

F/o.

Body

Round 1: mc 6. (6)

Round 2: (inc) 6 times. (12)

Round 3: (sc, inc) 6 times. (18)

Round 4: (2 sc, inc) 6 times. (24)

Round 5: (3 sc, inc) 6 times. (30)

Rounds 6–12: sc around. (30)

Round 13: (3 sc, dec) 6 times. (24)

Round 14: sc around. (24)

Round 15: (2 sc, dec) 6 times. (18)

Round 16: sc around. (18)

F/o, leaving a long tail for sewing.

(continued)

GRINDYLOW (CONTINUED)

Tentacles—Make 6

Round 1: mc 6. (6)

Round 2: sc around. (6)

Round 3: (2 sc, inc) 2 times. (8)

Round 4: sc around. (8)

Round 5: (3 sc, inc) 2 times. (10)

Rounds 6–7: sc around. (10)

Round 8: (4 sc, inc) 2 times. (12)

Rounds 9–11: sc around. (12)

Round 12: (5 sc, inc) 2 times. (14)

F/o, leaving a long tail for sewing.

Arms—Make 2

Starting with the first finger

Round 1: mc 6. (6)

Rounds 2–3: sc around. (6)

F/o.

Second finger

Round 1: mc 6. (6)

Rounds 2–3: sc around. (6)

Do not fasten off; join the next stitch into the first finger, and consider this the first stitch of Round 4.

Round 4: sc around. (12)

Round 5: (dec) 6 times. (6)

Rounds 6–9: sc around. (6)

F/o, leaving a long tail for sewing.

Head Tentacles—Make 2

Round 1: mc 6. (6)

Round 2: sc around. (6)

Round 3: (2 sc, inc) 2 times. (8)

Round 4: sc around. (8)

Round 5: (3 sc, inc) 2 times. (10)

Round 6: sc around. (10)

Round 7: (4 sc, inc) 2 times. (12)

Rounds 8–10: sc around. (12)

F/o, leaving a long tail for sewing.

Assembly

Whipstitch the bottom of the head closed. Stuff the body and attach it to the bottom of the head. Stuff each tentacle firmly and pin them, evenly spaced, going around the bottom of the body. Sew them on one by one, checking after each one you attach that your doll is still balanced. Next, attach the arms to either side of the body (no need to stuff them). Pin the head tentacles to either side of the face and sew them on (no need to stuff these either). Use the scissors to cut any leftover yarn tails from the limbs you've attached.

Finally, embroider the face details. Using your white yarn, embroider 4 top teeth and 4 bottom teeth in the center of the face. Using your black thread, embroider an outline of a mouth around the teeth. Finally, cut an extra strand of the soft green yarn, about 10 inches (25 cm) long, and embroider eye lids and a little nose. Your Grindylow is done!

KAPPA

Kappa are amphibious water demons from Japanese folklore. They are about the size of a human child, but they have much more scaly and turtle-like features. The most prominent feature—aside from its shell—is a flat indent on their head called a "dish." Its purpose is to retain water, or their life source, when they venture out of their water. If it dries up or spills while on land, they are in big trouble! I have to say, out of all the designs in this book, creating the Kappa was the most fun; this has to be my favorite design. I hope you like it as much as I do!

Head

In kiwi green

Round 1: mc 6. (6)

Round 2: (inc) 6 times. (12)

Round 3: (sc, inc) 6 times. (18)

Round 4: (2 sc, inc) 6 times. (24)

Round 5: (3 sc, inc) 6 times. (30)

Round 6: BLO (4 sc, inc) 6 times. (36)

Rounds 7–12: sc around. (36)

Round 13: (5 sc, inc) 6 times. (42)

Rounds 14–17: sc around. (42)

Pause crocheting here and cut two circles out of felt, approximately ½ inch (1.3 cm) in diameter. Cut a slit in the middle and insert an eye post into each circle, making the white circle the background of the eye. Trim your circle down so the top of the white circle is thinner (I make mine nearly invisible) and the bottom is wider. This will give your plush an adorable "looking up" expression.

(continued)

Abbreviations

BLO—crochet only in the back loop of the stitch for the following round

ch—chain

dec—invisible decrease

F/o—fasten off

FLO—crochet only in the front loop of the stitch for the following round

HDC—half double crochet

inc—increase or 2 single crochets in the same stitch

mc—magic circle

sc—single crochet

slpst—slip stitch

Materials Needed

- 4.0mm crochet hook (G hook)
- 1 (7-oz [198-g]) skein of medium worsted yarn in kiwi green (I used Premier® Yarns Everyday® Kiwi)
- 1 (7-oz [198-g]) skein of medium worsted yarn in dark green (I used Caron's Simply Soft Dark Sage)
- 1 (7-oz [198-g]) skein of medium worsted yarn in yellow (I used Big Twist's Value Pale Yellow)
- 1 (7-oz [198-g]) skein of medium worsted yarn in brown (I used Red Heart's Super Saver Coffee)
- 1 (7-oz [198-g]) skein of medium worsted yarn in white (I used Big Twist's Value White)
- 1 pair of 12mm safety eyes
- Fiberfill, for stuffing
- Tapestry needle
- Pins, to hold the limbs in place as you sew
- Scissors
- 1 sheet of white felt

KAPPA (CONTINUED)

When you're happy with your trimming, insert the eyes between Rounds 13 and 14 with 7 stitches in between them. Stuff the head firmly as you decrease.

Round 18: (5 sc, dec) 6 times. (36)

Round 19: (4 sc, dec) 6 times. (30)

Round 20: (3 sc, dec) 6 times. (24)

Round 21: (2 sc, dec) 6 times. (18)

Round 22: (sc, dec) 6 times. (12)

Round 23: (dec) 6 times. (6)

F/o.

Body

In kiwi green

Round 1: mc 6. (6)

Round 2: (inc) 6 times. (12)

Round 3: (sc, inc) 6 times. (18)

Round 4: (2 sc, inc) 6 times. (24)

Round 5: (3 sc, inc) 6 times. (30)

Round 6: (4 sc, inc) 6 times. (36)

Rounds 7–10: sc around. (36)

Round 11: (4 sc, dec) 6 times. (30)

Rounds 12–15: sc around. (30)

Round 16: (3 sc, dec) 6 times. (24)

Round 17: (2 sc, dec) 6 times. (18)

Round 18: (sc, dec) 6 times. (12)

F/o, leaving a long tail for sewing.

Legs—Make 2

In kiwi green

Round 1: mc 6. (6)

Round 2: (inc) 6 times. (12)

Round 3: (3 sc, inc) 3 times. (15)

Rounds 4–6: sc around. (15)

Round 7: (3 sc, dec) 3 times. (12)

Rounds 8–10: sc around. (12)

Round 11: (2 sc, dec) 3 times. (9)

Rounds 12–14: sc around. (9)

F/o, leaving a long tail for sewing.

Arms—Make 2

In kiwi green

Round 1: mc 6. (6)

Round 2: (inc) 6 times. (12)

Rounds 3–7: sc around. (12)

Round 8: (2 sc, dec) 3 times. (9)

Rounds 9–13: sc around. (9)

F/o, leaving a long tail for sewing.

Ears—Make 2

In kiwi green

Round 1: mc 6. (6)

Round 2: sc around. (6)

Round 3: (2 sc, inc) 2 times. (8)

Round 4: (3 sc, inc) 2 times. (10)

Round 5: (4 sc, inc) 2 times. (12)

Rounds 6–9: sc around. (12)

Round 10: (4 sc, dec) 2 times. (10)

F/o, leaving a long tail for sewing.

Tail

In kiwi green

Round 1: mc 4. (4)

Round 2: (sc, inc) 2 times. (6)

Round 3: (2 sc, inc) 2 times. (8)

Round 4: (3 sc, inc) 2 times. (10)

Rounds 5–6: sc around. (10)

F/o, leaving a long tail for sewing.

Leaves—Make 11

In dark green

Ch 4 and turn, put 2 HDC in the second chain from hook, sc in the next chain and slpst in the last. Ch 1 and turn the piece; you will now be crocheting down the other side, mirroring what you just did on the side you started with. Slpst in the same chain where you just did a slpst on the other side, sc in the next chain and put 2 HDC in the last.

F/o, leaving a long tail for sewing.

Beak

In yellow

Round 1: ch 4 and turn, sc around both sides of the chain (starting in the second chain from hook). (6)

Round 2: (sc, inc) 3 times. (9)

Round 3: (2 sc, inc) 3 times. (12)

Round 4: sc around. (12)

F/o, leaving a long tail for sewing.

Shell

In brown

Round 1: mc 6. (6)

Round 2: (inc) 6 times. (12)

Round 3: (sc, inc) 6 times. (18)

Rounds 4–5: sc around. (18)

Round 6: FLO HDC around. (18)

F/o, leaving a long tail for sewing.

Claws–Make 12

In white

Ch 3 and turn, slpst in the second chain from your hook, sc in the last chain.

F/o, leaving a long tail for sewing.

Assembly

Whipstitch the head closed. Stuff the body firmly and attach it to the bottom of the head. Stuff the legs, and attach them so your Kappa is in the "sitting" position. Lightly stuff the arms, concentrating most of the fluff in the bottom of the hands, and attach them to either side of the torso, right under where the head and body are attached.

Next, attach the tail to the back of the Kappa. If you are having slight balance problems with your Kappa's legs, the angle of the tail can be used to help correct that. Pin the shell to the middle of the back, and sew it on about 75 percent of the way. Pause here and stuff it; when it is firm enough, finish sewing it on. Next, attach the ears to either side of the head (no need to stuff them). Pin the beak to the middle of the face, in between the eyes, and sew it on when you are happy with its placement.

Attach the leaves around the top of the head where the ridge from the BLO stitches was formed. It took 11 leaves for me to completely cover the circumference. However, if your tension is looser, or you are working with a different type of yarn, you may need more or fewer leaves. I would recommend pinning them and making sure you have enough before starting to sew. If you just *barely* don't have enough leaves, you can play around with the spacing to see what your options are.

Finally, we're on the claws! Pin 3 claws to each limb (at the tip of each "foot" and "hand"). When you are happy with their spacing, sew them on. Use the scissors to cut any leftover yarn tails. With that final step, your Kappa is finished!

KAIJU

Kaiju come to us from Japanese folklore and mythology. They are fantastic and huge creatures that are said to hail from another dimension that can only be reached from the center of Earth. They can come in so many forms and have so many different abilities, but one thing they all have in common is that the word "titan" could definitely be used to describe them! I chose to go with an ocean-dwelling one who can swim faster than anything our world has seen, but it can also stomp around on land, crushing cities beneath its feet. However, our Kaiju is very good, and wouldn't do the latter!

Materials Needed

- 4.0mm crochet hook (G hook)
- 1 (7-oz [198-g]) skein of medium worsted yarn in dark blue (I used Caron's One Pound Midnight Blue)
- 1 (7-oz [198-g]) skein of medium worsted yarn in light blue (I used Caron's Simply Soft Soft Blue)
- 1 pair of 12mm safety eyes
- Fiberfill, for stuffing
- Tapestry needle
- Pins, to hold the limbs in place as you sew
- Scissors
- 1 sheet of white felt

Abbreviations

dec–invisible decrease

F/o–fasten off

inc–increase or 2 single crochets in the same stitch

mc–magic circle

sc–single crochet

Head

In dark blue

Round 1: mc 6. (6)

Round 2: (inc) 6 times. (12)

Round 3: (sc, inc) 6 times. (18)

Round 4: (2 sc, inc) 6 times. (24)

Round 5: (3 sc, inc) 6 times. (30)

Round 6: (4 sc, inc) 6 times. (36)

Rounds 7–10: sc around. (36)

Round 11: 6 sc, 6 inc, 24 sc. (42)

Round 12: 6 sc, (sc, inc) 6 times, 24 sc. (48)

Rounds 13–16: sc around. (48)

Pause crocheting here and cut 2 circles out of felt, approximately ½ inch (1.3 cm) in diameter. Cut a slit in the middle and insert an eye post into each circle, making the white circle the background of the eye. Trim your circle down so the top of the white circle is thinner (I make mine nearly invisible) and the bottom is wider. This will give your plush an adorable "looking up" expression. When you're happy with your trimming, insert the eyes between Rounds 11 and 12 with 15 stitches in between them (place them on either side of the increases).

Round 17: (6 sc, dec) 6 times. (42)

Round 18: (5 sc, dec) 6 times. (36)

Round 19: (4 sc, dec) 6 times. (30)

Round 20: (3 sc, dec) 6 times. (24)

Round 21: (2 sc, dec) 6 times. (18)

Round 22: (sc, dec) 6 times. (12)

Round 23: (dec) 6 times. (6)

Stuff the head firmly as you decrease.

(continued)

KAIJU (CONTINUED)

Body

In dark blue

Round 1: mc 6. (6)

Round 2: (inc) 6 times. (12)

Round 3: (sc, inc) 6 times. (18)

Round 4: (2 sc, inc) 6 times. (24)

Round 5: (3 sc, inc) 6 times. (30)

Round 6: (4 sc, inc) 6 times. (36)

Round 7: (5 sc, inc) 6 times. (42)

Rounds 8–11: sc around. (42)

Round 12: (5 sc, dec) 6 times. (36)

Rounds 13–16: sc around. (36)

Round 17: (4 sc, dec) 6 times. (30)

Rounds 18–20: sc around. (30)

Round 21: (3 sc, dec) 6 times. (24)

Round 22: sc around. (24)

Round 23: (2 sc, dec) 6 times. (18)

F/o, leaving a long tail for sewing.

Tail

In dark blue

Round 1: mc 6. (6)

Round 2: sc around. (6)

Round 3: (2 sc, inc) 2 times. (8)

Round 4: sc around. (8)

Round 5: (3 sc, inc) 2 times. (10)

Round 6: sc around. (10)

Round 7: (4 sc, inc) 2 times. (12)

Round 8: sc around. (12)

Round 9: (5 sc, inc) 2 times. (14)

Round 10: sc around. (14)

Round 11: (6 sc, inc) 2 times. (16)

Round 12: sc around. (16)

Round 13: (7 sc, inc) 2 times. (18)

Round 14: sc around. (18)

Round 15: (8 sc, inc) 2 times. (20)

Round 16: sc around. (20)

Round 17: (9 sc, inc) 2 times. (22)

Round 18: sc around. (22)

Round 19: (10 sc, inc) 2 times. (24)

Round 20: sc around. (24)

Round 21: (11 sc, inc) 2 times. (26)

Round 22: sc around. (26)

F/o, leaving a long tail for sewing.

Haunches—Make 2

In dark blue

Round 1: mc 6. (6)

Round 2: (inc) 6 times. (12)

Round 3: (sc, inc) 6 times. (18)

Round 4: (2 sc, inc) 6 times. (24)

Round 5: (3 sc, inc) 6 times. (30)

Rounds 6–10: sc around. (30)

Round 11: (3 sc, dec) 6 times. (24)

Round 12: (2 sc, dec) 6 times. (18)

Round 13: (sc, dec) 6 times. (12)

Round 14: (dec) 6 times. (6)

F/o, leaving a long tail for sewing.

Feet—Make 2

In dark blue

Round 1: mc 6. (6)

Round 2: (inc) 6 times. (12)

Rounds 3–6: sc around. (12)

F/o, leaving a long tail for sewing.

Arms—Make 2

In dark blue

Round 1: mc 6. (6)

Round 2: (sc, inc) 3 times. (9)

Rounds 3–12: sc around. (9)

F/o, leaving a long tail for sewing.

Spikes—Make 6

In light blue

Round 1: mc 6. (6)

Round 2: sc around. (6)

Round 3: (2 sc, inc) 2 times. (8)

Round 4: sc around. (8)

Round 5: (3 sc, inc) 2 times. (10)

Round 6: sc around. (10)

F/o, leaving a long tail for sewing.

Assembly

Whipstitch the head closed. Stuff the body firmly and attach it to the bottom of the head. Next, stuff the haunches. You want them to be stuffed enough to hold their shape, but empty enough to sew on with a side flatly placed against the body. Attach them to either side of the body. Next, lightly stuff the feet and attach them under the haunches.

Next, stuff the tail and attach it to the back of the body. Sew it on at a downward angle, so it's used to balance the body. Pin the arms to either side of the body, and attach them right under where the head and the body are sewn together. Finally, attach the spikes, evenly spaced, starting at the top of the head, to the tip of the tail. Use the scissors to cut any leftover yarn tails. Now your Kaiju is finished!

Chapter 4

FOREST DWELLERS

It's quiet in the forest, you are surrounded by trees older than cities and moss thicker than crowded on-ramps, and the air is fresher than an October morning. There is a magic to it, standing in nature, a magic that could almost allow you to believe that, in this particular forest, you will find all sorts of things that you don't see in your daily life, from a quiet Centaur (page 90) to a protective Leshy (page 99) and maybe some elusive Gnomes (page 87) or even Big Foot himself (page 85). Embrace the magic, gather your yarn and see what this chapter has to hold!

BIG FOOT

Being born and raised in the Pacific Northwest myself, I can assure you people believe in Big Foot around there! He is a giant ape-like creature who resides in the U.S. West Coast's deep forests. He leads a very solitary life, and he gets upset when he has to deal with people trying to find him, photograph him or worse—hunt him! Can you blame the guy? He is known to throw rocks and exhibit quite territorial behaviors, so if you find your crochet Big Foot is a bit moody, try giving him a little space! He should calm down when he feels less threatened. I suggest using a super fluffy type of yarn when making this guy to make him extra cuddly, but if you don't have access to such a yarn, you can always use regular worsted yarn and the "brushing out" technique we used when making the Werewolf (page 37).

(page 37)

Materials Needed

- 4.0mm crochet hook (G hook)
- 1 (7-oz [198-g]) skein of medium worsted yarn in preferred skin tone (I used Red Heart's Super Saver Buff)
- 1 (7-oz [198-g]) skein of fluffy bulky weight yarn in brown (I used Bernat's Pipsqueak™ Chocolate)
- 1 pair of 12mm safety eyes
- Fiberfill, for stuffing
- Tapestry needle
- Pins, to hold the limbs in place as you sew
- Scissors
- Black embroidery floss

Abbreviations

ch—chain
dec—invisible decrease
F/o—fasten off
inc—increase or 2 single crochets in the same stitch
mc—magic circle
sc—single crochet

Head

In preferred skin tone

Round 1: ch 7, turn and sc around foundation chain (putting 2 stitches in each end of the chain). (12)

Round 2: (sc, inc) 6 times. (18)

Round 3: (2 sc, inc) 6 times. (24)

Round 4: (3 sc, inc) 6 times. (30)

Round 5: (4 sc, inc) 6 times. (36)

Change to brown fluffy yarn

Round 6: (5 sc, inc) 6 times. (42)

Rounds 7–14: sc around. (42)

Insert the eyes between Rounds 2 and 3 with 7 stitches between them. Stuff the head firmly as you decrease.

Round 15: (5 sc, dec) 6 times. (36)

Round 16: (4 sc, dec) 6 times. (30)

Round 17: (3 sc, dec) 6 times. (24)

Round 18: (2 sc, dec) 6 times. (18)

Round 19: (sc, dec) 6 times. (12)

Round 20: (dec) 6 times. (6)

F/o.

(continued)

BIG FOOT (CONTINUED)

Body

In brown fluffy yarn

Round 1: mc 6. (6)

Round 2: (inc) 6 times. (12)

Round 3: (sc, inc) 6 times. (18)

Round 4: (2 sc, inc) 6 times. (24)

Round 5: (3 sc, inc) 6 times. (30)

Round 6: (4 sc, inc) 6 times. (36)

Round 7: (5 sc, inc) 6 times. (42)

Rounds 8–11: sc around. (42)

Round 12: (5 sc, dec) 6 times. (36)

Round 13: sc around. (36)

Round 14: (4 sc, dec) 6 times. (30)

Round 15: sc around. (30)

Round 16: (3 sc, dec) 6 times. (24)

Round 17: sc around. (24)

Round 18: (2 sc, dec) 6 times. (18)

Rounds 19–20: sc around. (18)

Round 21: (sc, dec) 6 times. (12)

Round 22: sc around. (12)

F/o, leaving a long tail for sewing.

Arms–Make 2

In preferred skin tone

Round 1: mc 6. (6)

Round 2: (inc) 6 times. (12)

Round 3: (sc, inc) 6 times. (18)

Round 4: sc around. (18)

Change to brown fluffy yarn

Rounds 5–7: sc around. (18)

Round 8: (3 sc, dec) 3 times. (15)

Rounds 9–15: sc around. (15)

F/o, leaving a long tail for sewing.

Legs–Make 2

In preferred skin tone

Round 1: mc 6. (6)

Round 2: (inc) 6 times. (12)

Round 3: (sc, inc) 6 times. (18)

Round 4: (2 sc, inc) 6 times. (24)

Round 5: (3 sc, inc) 6 times. (30)

Round 6: sc around. (30)

Change to brown fluffy yarn

Rounds 7–9: sc around. (30)

Round 10: (3 sc, dec) 6 times. (24)

Rounds 11–13: sc around. (24)

Round 14: (2 sc, dec) 6 times. (18)

Rounds 15–17: sc around. (18)

Round 18: (sc, dec) 6 times. (12)

Rounds 19–21: sc around. (12)

F/o, leaving a long tail for sewing.

Assembly

First of all, take a minute to congratulate yourself. Working with fluffy yarn is *not* easy! Well done for keeping your cool and getting this far! Now, on to the assembly. Whipstitch the head closed, then stuff the body firmly and attach it to the bottom of the head. Stuff the legs firmly and attach them to the body, so your Big Foot is in a sitting position. Next, attach the arms to either side of the body, in line with where the head and the body are sewn together (no need to stuff the arms). Use the scissors to cut any leftover yarn tails from the limbs you've attached. Lastly, embroider a little smile with some black embroidery floss. With this, your Big Foot is done!

If you have trouble working with fluffy yarn, another option is to crochet him entirely with regular acrylic yarn and then brush out the fur portions with a metal pet brush. (See the Werewolf pattern [page 37] to reference how to brush out the yarn to give it a fluffy look and feel.) You could also use white fluffy yarn and light blue acrylic yarn to turn this same pattern into an Abominable Snowman! I hope you have fun with this one and any other renditions you choose to make!

GNOME

Gnomes live deep in the forest and seldom come into contact with humans. Despite their tiny stature, they can be up to seven times stronger than the average human, and they can run up to 35 miles per hour! They are vegetarians who are known for being guardians of the forest. They spend much of their time caring for animals, freeing those who are trapped in hunting snares and sneakily tending to neglected farm animals. However, their greatest enemy are cats, both wild and domesticated. So, keep this in mind as you make your Gnomes if you have a feline friend! These little guys are super quick makes; you'll be able to create so many in no time!

Head

In preferred skin tone

Round 1: mc 6. (6)

Round 2: (inc) 6 times. (12)

Round 3: (sc, inc) 6 times. (18)

Round 4: (2 sc, inc) 6 times. (24)

Round 5: (3 sc, inc) 6 times. (30)

Round 6: (4 sc, inc) 6 times. (36)

Rounds 7–15: sc around. (36)

Round 16: (4 sc, dec) 6 times. (30)

Round 17: (3 sc, dec) 6 times. (24)

Stuff the head firmly as you continue to decrease.

Round 18: (2 sc, dec) 6 times. (18)

Round 19: (sc, dec) 6 times. (12)

Round 20: (dec) 6 times. (6)

F/o.

Nose

In preferred skin tone

Round 1: mc 6. (6)

Round 2: (inc) 6 times. (12)

Round 3: (3 sc, inc) 3 times. (15)

Round 4: sc around. (15)

Round 5: (3 sc, dec) 3 times. (12)

Round 6: (2 sc, dec) 3 times. (9)

(continued)

Materials Needed

- 4.0mm crochet hook (G hook)
- 1 (7-oz [198-g]) skein of medium worsted yarn in preferred skin tone (I used Red Heart's Super Saver Buff)
- 1 (7-oz [198-g]) skein of medium worsted yarn in red (I used Big Twist's Value Red)
- 1 (7-oz [198-g]) skein of medium worsted yarn in dark blue (I used Caron's One Pound Midnight Blue)
- 1 (7-oz [198-g]) skein of medium worsted yarn in white (I used Big Twist's Value White)
- Fiberfill, for stuffing
- Tapestry needle
- Pins, to hold the limbs in place as you sew
- Scissors

Abbreviations

dec–invisible decrease

F/o–fasten off

inc–increase or 2 single crochets in the same stitch

mc–magic circle

sc–single crochet

GNOME (CONTINUED)

Hat

In red

Round 1: mc 4. (4)

Round 2: (sc, inc) 2 times. (6)

Round 3: (2 sc, inc) 2 times. (8)

Round 4: (3 sc, inc) 2 times. (10)

Round 5: sc around. (10)

Round 6: (4 sc, inc) 2 times. (12)

Round 7: sc around. (12)

Round 8: (3 sc, inc) 3 times. (15)

Round 9: sc around. (15)

Round 10: (4 sc, inc) 3 times. (18)

Round 11: sc around. (18)

Round 12: (5 sc, inc) 3 times. (21)

Round 13: sc around. (21)

Round 14: (6 sc, inc) 3 times. (24)

Round 15: sc around. (24)

Round 16: (3 sc, inc) 6 times. (30)

Round 17: sc around. (30)

Round 18: (4 sc, inc) 6 times. (36)

Round 19: sc around. (36)

Round 20: (5 sc, inc) 6 times. (42)

Rounds 21–23: sc around. (42)

F/o, leaving a long tail for sewing.

Body

In dark blue

Round 1: mc 6. (6)

Round 2: (inc) 6 times. (12)

Round 3: (sc, inc) 6 times. (18)

Round 4: (2 sc, inc) 6 times. (24)

Round 5: (3 sc, inc) 6 times. (30)

Round 6: (4 sc, inc) 6 times. (36)

Rounds 7–9: sc around. (36)

Round 10: (4 sc, dec) 6 times. (30)

Rounds 11–12: sc around. (30)

Round 13: (3 sc, dec) 6 times. (24)

Round 14: sc around. (24)

Round 15: (2 sc, dec) 6 times. (18)

Round 16: sc around. (18)

Round 17: (sc, dec) 6 times. (12)

F/o, leaving a long tail for sewing.

Assembly

Whipstitch the head closed, then stuff the body firmly and attach it to the bottom of the head. Stuff the nose and sew it to the middle of the face. Next, begin stuffing the hat, making sure you get the tip of it nice and firm. Pull the hat over the head; it should go about halfway down (resting on the nose) and sew it on. Use the scissors to cut any leftover yarn tails from the pieces you've attached.

For the beard, cut about 40 (6-inch [15-cm]) strands of white yarn and attach them via the latch hook method around and under the nose. Once the beard is nice and full, carefully trim it to your desired length. When you're happy with the way it looks, your Gnome is done!

CENTAUR

Centaurs are noble and proud creatures who lead quiet lives in the forest. They live together in herds, are family-oriented and are skilled at healing, astrology and archery. These half-human, half-horse creatures are prominent in Greek mythology and many modern fantasy tales. With the following pattern, you can make your own Centaur! Don't be intimidated by the idea of having to balance your doll just perfectly before sewing him together to get a standing position, because in this pattern I suggest an adorable laying down pose. This is much easier to sew and just as cute! If you are up for the challenge, you absolutely can attempt the traditional standing position, but if you are a beginner, or just don't feel like it, this is an excellent alternative that I often use when making four-legged dolls.

Head

In preferred skin tone

Round 1: mc 6. (6)

Round 2: (inc) 6 times. (12)

Round 3: (sc, inc) 6 times. (18)

Round 4: (2 sc, inc) 6 times. (24)

Round 5: (3 sc, inc) 6 times. (30)

Round 6: (4 sc, inc) 6 times. (36)

Rounds 7–15: sc around. (36)

Insert the eyes between Rounds 11 and 12 with 6 stitches in between. Start stuffing the head as you decrease.

Round 16: (4 sc, dec) 6 times. (30)

Round 17: (3 sc, dec) 6 times. (24)

Round 18: (2 sc, dec) 6 times. (18)

Round 19: (sc, dec) 6 times. (12)

Round 20: (dec) 6 times. (6)

F/o.

Wig Cap

In black

Round 1: mc 6. (6)

Round 2: (inc) 6 times. (12)

Round 3: (sc, inc) 6 times. (18)

Round 4: (2 sc, inc) 6 times. (24)

Round 5: (3 sc, inc) 6 times. (30)

Round 6: (4 sc, inc) 6 times. (36)

Rounds 7–11: sc around. (36)

F/o, leaving a long tail for sewing.

Materials Needed

- 4.0mm crochet hook (G hook)
- 1 (7-oz [198-g]) skein of medium worsted yarn in preferred skin tone (I used Red Heart's Super Saver Buff)
- 1 (7-oz [198-g]) skein of medium worsted yarn in black (I used Caron's Simply Soft Black)
- 1 (7-oz [198-g]) skein of medium worsted yarn in dark brown (I used Big Twist's Value Chocolate)
- 1 pair of 9mm safety eyes
- Fiberfill, for stuffing
- Tapestry needle
- Pins, to hold the limbs in place as you sew
- Scissors
- Fabri-Tac glue or hot glue

Abbreviations

dec—invisible decrease

F/o—fasten off

inc—increase or 2 single crochets in the same stitch

mc—magic circle

sc—single crochet

Ears–Make 2

In preferred skin tone

Round 1: mc 5. (5)

Smoosh all stitches to one side of the magic circle to create a semi-circle.

F/o, leaving a long tail for sewing.

Torso

In dark brown

Round 1: mc 6. (6)

Round 2: (inc) 6 times. (12)

Round 3: (sc, inc) 6 times. (18)

Round 4: (2 sc, inc) 6 times. (24)

Round 5: (3 sc, inc) 6 times. (30)

Rounds 6–11: sc around. (30)

Change to preferred skin tone

Round 12: sc around. (30)

Round 13: (3 sc, dec) 6 times. (24)

Rounds 14–16: sc around. (24)

Round 17: (2 sc, dec) 6 times. (18)

Rounds 18–19: sc around. (18)

Round 20: (sc, dec) 6 times. (12)

Round 21: sc around. (12)

F/o, leaving a long tail for sewing.

Body

In dark brown

Round 1: mc 6. (6)

Round 2: (inc) 6 times. (12)

Round 3: (sc, inc) 6 times. (18)

Round 4: (2 sc, inc) 6 times. (24)

Round 5: (3 sc, inc) 6 times. (30)

Rounds 6–11: sc around. (30)

Round 12: (3 sc, dec) 6 times. (24)

Rounds 13–16: sc around. (24)

F/o, leaving a long tail for sewing.

Legs–Make 4

In black

Round 1: mc 6. (6)

Round 2: (inc) 6 times. (12)

Round 3: (3 sc, inc) 3 times. (15)

Rounds 4–5: sc around. (15)

Round 6: (3 sc, dec) 3 times. (12)

Change to dark brown

Rounds 7–9: sc around. (12)

Round 10: (2 sc, dec) 3 times. (9)

Rounds 11–15: sc around. (9)

F/o, leaving a long tail for sewing.

(continued)

CENTAUR (CONTINUED)

Arms—Make 2

In preferred skin tone

Round 1: mc 6. (6)

Round 2: (sc, inc) 3 times. (9)

Rounds 3–4: sc around. (9)

Round 5: (sc, dec) 3 times. (6)

Rounds 6–9: sc around. (6)

F/o, leaving a long tail for sewing.

Assembly

Whipstitch the head closed. Stuff the torso firmly and attach it to the bottom of the head. Next, stuff the body and attach it to the bottom back of the torso. Try your best to align the top of the body to where the dark brown of the torso ends; this will help make it look like it is one flowing piece. Next, stuff the legs and attach 2 to either side of the bottom of the torso, and 2 to either side of the back of the body. I chose to make my Centaur in a sitting position, so I sewed them on horizontally. This is my preferred style, but if you want yours to be standing on all fours, just remember to check for balance after each leg is attached! Next, attach the arms to either side of the top of the torso, right under the head (no need to stuff them). Use the scissors to cut any leftover yarn tails from the limbs you've attached.

Now it is time for the head details. First, attach the ears to either side of the head in line with the eyes. Sew the wig cap on the top of the head, and use the remaining yarn tail to embroider sideburns in front of each ear. I didn't have enough yarn leftover to do the hair once this was done, so I cut a new strand of black yarn about 10 inches (25 cm) long and wove it through the piece to the front of the wig cap (where we will begin attaching the hair). Cut about 40 strands of black yarn that are about 8 inches (20 cm) long. Begin sewing bundles of 4 to the top of the head, using the 10-inch (25-cm) strand of black yarn. Keep sewing bundles as you work your way to the back of the head. Try to keep your sewing line straight, as this will be where the hair parts; also pull *very* tightly when you are sewing them down to make sure they are extra secure. Once you have enough bundles to fill your head of hair, you can secure the strands even more by applying a thin line of glue to either side of the part, under the hair. Remember, a little bit of glue goes a long way! Next, trim your hair to your desired length. Take it slow—you can't undo cutting the hair too short!

Finally, make a tail by latch hooking a bundle of 3 (6-inch [15-cm]) strands of black yarn. Pull tight to secure and trim to your desired length. Your Centaur is now done!

CHIMERA

The Chimera is one of the most fantastic monsters in Greek mythology. A Chimera is a fire-breathing lion with the heads of a goat and a dragon, and a serpent's tail. It doesn't get more epic than this! They reside in montane forests and come down to swipe sheep and cattle from nearby farms for food. This pattern is a sewing marathon, but it's unlike anything out there. It is the most perfect gift for someone who is obsessed with mythology. Trust in the process—this is an awesome piece!

Body

In beige

Round 1: mc 6. (6)

Round 2: (inc) 6 times. (12)

Round 3: (sc, inc) 6 times. (18)

Round 4: (2 sc, inc) 6 times. (24)

Round 5: (3 sc, inc) 6 times. (30)

Round 6: (4 sc, inc) 6 times. (36)

Rounds 7–25: sc around. (36)

Round 26: (4 sc, dec) 6 times. (30)

Round 27: (3 sc, dec) 6 times. (24)

Stuff firmly as you continue to decrease.

Round 28: (2 sc, dec) 6 times. (18)

Round 29: (sc, dec) 6 times. (12)

Round 30: (dec) 6 times. (6)

F/o, leaving a long tail for sewing.

Abbreviations

ch—chain

dec—invisible decrease

F/o—fasten off

FLO—crochet only in the front loop of the stitch for the following round

HDC—half double crochet

inc—increase or 2 single crochets in the same stitch

mc—magic circle

sc—single crochet

slpst—slip stitch

Materials Needed

- 4.0mm crochet hook (G hook)
- 1 (7-oz [198-g]) skein of medium worsted yarn in beige (I used Red Heart's Super Saver Buff)
- 1 (7-oz [198-g]) skein of medium worsted yarn in red (I used Red Heart's Super Saver Cherry Red)
- 1 (7-oz [198-g]) skein of medium worsted yarn in black (I used Caron's Simply Soft Black)
- 1 (7-oz [198-g]) skein of medium worsted yarn in grey (I used I Love This Yarn's Graymist)
- 1 (7-oz [198-g]) skein of medium worsted yarn in green (I used I Love This Yarn's Light Sage)
- 1 (7-oz [198-g]) skein of medium worsted yarn in brown (I used Big Twist's Value Chocolate)
- 3 pairs of 12mm safety eyes
- 1 pair of 6mm safety eyes
- Fiberfill, for stuffing
- Tapestry needle
- Pins, to hold the limbs in place as you sew
- Scissors
- 1 (12-inch [30-cm]) crafting pipe cleaner

Lion's Head

In beige

Round 1: mc 6. (6)

Round 2: (inc) 6 times. (12)

Round 3: (sc, inc) 6 times. (18)

Round 4: (2 sc, inc) 6 times. (24)

Round 5: (3 sc, inc) 6 times. (30)

Round 6: (4 sc, inc) 6 times. (36)

Rounds 7–13: sc around. (36)

Round 14: (5 sc, inc) 6 times. (42)

Rounds 15–17: sc around. (42)

Place a pair of 12mm eyes between Rounds 12 and 13 with 7 stitches in between. Stuff the head firmly as you decrease.

Round 18: (5 sc, dec) 6 times. (36)

Round 19: (4 sc, dec) 6 times. (30)

Round 20: (3 sc, dec) 6 times. (24)

Round 21: (2 sc, dec) 6 times. (18)

Round 22: (sc, dec) 6 times. (12)

Round 23: (dec) 6 times. (6)

F/o.

Lion's Muzzle

In beige

Round 1: mc 6. (6)

Round 2: (inc) 6 times. (12)

Round 3: (sc, inc) 6 times. (18)

Rounds 4–7: sc around. (18)

F/o, leaving a long tail for sewing.

Lion's Ears—Make 2

In beige

Round 1: mc 6. (6)

Round 2: (inc) 6 times. (12)

Rounds 3–5: sc around. (12)

F/o, leaving a long tail for sewing.

Dragon's Head

In red

Round 1: mc 6. (6)

Round 2: (inc) 6 times. (12)

Round 3: (sc, inc) 6 times. (18)

Round 4: (2 sc, inc) 6 times. (24)

Rounds 5–7: sc around. (24)

Round 8: 6 sc, (FLO inc) 6 times, 12 sc. (30)

Round 9: 9 sc, 6 inc, 15 sc. (36)

Rounds 10–16: sc around. (36)

Place a pair of 12mm eyes between Rounds 8 and 9 with 11 stitches in between (center the snout between them). Stuff the head firmly as you decrease.

Round 17: (dec) 3 times, 24 sc, (dec) 3 times. (30)

Round 18: (dec) 3 times, 18 sc, (dec) 3 times. (24)

Round 19: (2 sc, dec) 6 times. (18)

Rounds 20–25: sc around. (18)

F/o, leaving a long tail for sewing.

Dragon's Horns—Make 2

In black

Round 1: mc 6. (6)

Rounds 2–5: sc around. (6)

F/o, leaving a long tail for sewing.

(continued)

CHIMERA (CONTINUED)

Dragon's Ears–Make 2

In red

Ch 4 and turn, starting in the chain closest to your hook: slpst, sc in the next stitch, HDC in the last stitch.

F/o, leaving a long tail for sewing.

Goat's Head

In grey

Round 1: mc 6. (6)

Round 2: (inc) 6 times. (12)

Round 3: (sc, inc) 6 times. (18)

Round 4: (2 sc, inc) 6 times. (24)

Round 5: (3 sc, inc) 6 times. (30)

Round 6: (4 sc, inc) 6 times. (36)

Rounds 7–12: sc around. (36)

Round 13: (5 sc, inc) 6 times. (42)

Rounds 14–16: sc around. (42)

Insert a pair of 12mm eyes between Rounds 11 and 12 with 7 stitches in between. Stuff the head firmly as you decrease.

Round 17: (5 sc, dec) 6 times. (36)

Round 18: (4 sc, dec) 6 times. (30)

Round 19: (3 sc, dec) 6 times. (24)

Round 20: (2 sc, dec) 6 times. (18)

Round 21: (sc, dec) 6 times. (12)

Round 22: (dec) 6 times. (6)

F/o.

Goat's Ears–Make 2

In grey

Round 1: mc 6. (6)

Round 2: (inc) 6 times. (12)

Round 3: (sc, inc) 6 times. (18)

Fold the ear in half, turn, (no need to chain up) sc to the other side. (9)

F/o, leaving a long tail for sewing.

Goat's Muzzle

In grey

Round 1: ch 7, turn and sc around the foundation chain (putting 2 stitches in each end of the chain). (12)

Round 2: (sc, inc) 6 times. (18)

Rounds 3–4: sc around. (18)

F/o, leaving a long tail for sewing.

Goat's Horns–Make 2

In black

Round 1: mc 6. (6)

Rounds 2–5: sc around. (6)

F/o, leaving a long tail for sewing.

Legs–Make 4

In beige

Round 1: mc 6. (6)

Round 2: (inc) 6 times. (12)

Round 3: (sc, inc) 6 times. (18)

Round 4: (2 sc, inc) 6 times. (24)

Rounds 5–8: sc around. (24)

Round 9: (dec) 6 times, 12 sc. (18)

Rounds 10–16: sc around. (18)

F/o, leaving a long tail for sewing.

Serpent Tail

In green

Round 1: mc 6. (6)

Round 2: (inc) 6 times. (12)

Rounds 3–5: sc around. (12)

Insert the 6mm eyes between Rounds 3 and 4 with 5 stitches in between.

Round 6: (2 sc, dec) 3 times. (9)

Round 7: (sc, dec) 3 times. (6)

There is no need to stuff the serpent's head. Insert the pipe cleaner into the head and continue crocheting around it as you finish the serpent. I cut my pipe cleaner to be about 6 inches (15 cm) long. With my tension, I end up with 36 to 37 rounds. You may have more or less depending on how tightly you crochet and what type of yarn you're using. When you reach the end of the pipe cleaner, F/o your yarn and leave a long tail for sewing the serpent tail to the body.

(continued)

CHIMERA (CONTINUED)

Assembly

Whipstitch the lion's head closed, and attach the muzzle to the center of the face (stuffing as you sew) and the ears to the top of the head. Next use black yarn and embroider a nose on the top of the muzzle. Use the long yarn tail from the body and attach the head to the top of the body. Sew it on very tightly because by the end, the Chimera is going to be very heavy! (Don't cut the tail from the body yet; we will use it to attach the goat's head too.)

Once you have the lion's head on well, we are going to begin filling in the mane. Cut about 100 (3-inch [8-cm]) strands of brown yarn. Begin filling in the mane using the latch hook method. Once the mane is full enough, begin trimming the hair. Be very careful—the mane is a lot of work and you don't want to cut too short accidentally and have to pull some out to restart a section!

Next, stuff the dragon's neck firmly; we want it to be able to hold its shape and stand on its own. Use the yarn tail from the neck and attach it to the left of the lion's head. I tucked mine as close to the mane as I could. (The goal is to have all the heads as close to the front of the body as possible.) Then, attach the horns to the top of the head and the ears to either side of those. Use a strand of red yarn to embroider eyelids over the eyes to make the dragon look a bit more fierce.

Now it's time for the goat. Whipstitch the bottom of the goat's head closed. Attach the muzzle (stuffing as you sew). Embroider a nose and mouth with black yarn. Next, attach the horns to the top of the head and the ears to either side of them. Use the yarn tail from the body to attach the head to the right of the lion. Again, make sure you sew it on very tightly!

Stuff all 4 legs and attach them to the body. I used the front 2 to help balance the doll as it is very front-heavy! Play around with positioning and see what style/positioning works best for your doll.

Finally, we can finish the serpent tail. Whipstitch the bottom of the serpent closed and attach him to the back of the Chimera. I wanted mine to be in the upward position and pointing forward. Play around with yours to see how you would like it—the pipe cleaner inside gives us endless possibilities! Use the scissors to cut off any leftover yarn tails. With that, your Chimera is done!

LESHY

Leshy is a forest spirit from Slavic mythology who protects animals, forests and marshes. He is mostly benevolent, unless someone enters the forest with sinister intentions. In that case, he may or may not tap into his trickster ways, and the previously considered "guests" will now be considered intruders and will be treated as such! You can create your own little forest guardian with this pattern. May he always look after those in need, including you! In this pattern, we use felt to create "leafy" details. I know it can be a bit tedious to cut out so many little pieces, but the more layers you apply and time you spend constructing him, the more awesome he will turn out!

Head

In white

Round 1: mc 6. (6)

Round 2: (inc) 6 times. (12)

Round 3: (sc, inc) 6 times. (18)

Round 4: (2 sc, inc) 6 times. (24)

Round 5: (3 sc, inc) 6 times. (30)

Round 6: (4 sc, inc) 6 times. (36)

Rounds 7–15: sc around. (36)

Round 16: (4 sc, dec) 6 times. (30)

Round 17: (3 sc, dec) 6 times. (24)

Stuff firmly as you continue to decrease.

Round 18: (2 sc, dec) 6 times. (18)

Round 19: (sc, dec) 6 times. (12)

Round 20: (dec) 6 times. (6)

F/o.

Snout

In white

Round 1: mc 6. (6)

Round 2: (inc) 6 times. (12)

Round 3: sc around. (12)

Round 4: (3 sc, inc) 3 times. (15)

Rounds 5–6: sc around. (15)

Round 7: (4 sc, inc) 3 times. (18)

Rounds 8–9: sc around. (18)

F/o, leaving a long tail for sewing.

Body

Starting with the first leg, in light green

Round 1: mc 6. (6)

Round 2: (inc) 6 times. (12)

Rounds 3–7: sc around. (12)

F/o.

(continued)

LESHY (CONTINUED)

Second leg, in light green

Round 1: mc 6. (6)

Round 2: (inc) 6 times. (12)

Rounds 3–7: sc around. (12)

Do not fasten off; join the next stitch into the first leg, and consider this the first stitch of Round 8.

Round 8: sc around. (24)

Rounds 9–15: sc around. (24)

Round 16: (2 sc, dec) 6 times. (18)

Round 17: sc around. (18)

Round 18: (sc, dec) 6 times. (12)

F/o, leaving a long tail for sewing.

Arms—Make 2

In light green

Round 1: mc 6. (6)

Round 2: (sc, inc) 3 times. (9)

Rounds 3–9: sc around. (9)

F/o, leaving a long tail for sewing.

Large Antler—Make 2

In brown

Round 1: mc 6. (6)

Round 2: (sc, inc) 3 times. (9)

Rounds 3–14: sc around. (9)

Change to white

Round 15: sc around. (9)

F/o, leaving a long tail for sewing.

Small Antler—Make 2

In brown

Round 1: mc 6. (6)

Round 2: (sc, inc) 3 times. (9)

Rounds 3–5: sc around. (9)

F/o, leaving a long tail for sewing.

Assembly

Whipstitch the head closed, then stuff the body firmly and attach it to the bottom of the head. Attach the arms to either side of the body. Stuff the large antler pieces, and sew them to either side of the top of the head. Next, stuff the small antler pieces and attach 1 to the inside of each of the large antler pieces. Stuff the snout and attach it to the middle of the head, a little below the center line. Use the scissors to cut any leftover yarn tails.

Cut black eyes out of felt, and glue them to either side of the snout. Mine came out to be 1 inch (2.5 cm) long and ½ inch (1.3 cm) tall. Please refer to my finished doll's picture for shaping. Next, cut two little half circles out of black felt and glue them next to each other on the center of the snout. Each of mine were ½ inch (1.3 cm) in diameter and ¼ inch (6 mm) in height. *Please note: these measurements are based on the final size of my doll; depending on your tension you may require larger or smaller felt pieces to maintain the same proportions.*

For the leafy chest piece, cut about 40 small leaf shapes out of green felt. I cut mine to be ½ inch (1.3 cm) long and ¼ inch (6 mm) wide. Begin gluing leaves at the top of the torso, going over the shoulders of the doll, then work your way down, layering them as you go. I only attached leaves to the front of my doll and stopped about halfway down the chest, but you can add as many or as few leaves as you would like. Once your glue has dried, your Leshy is done!

JERSEY DEVIL

In the Pinelands of southern New Jersey resides the most infamous cryptid of the U.S. East Coast—the Jersey Devil. He's been prowling for over 250 years, with eyewitness accounts and the aftermaths of his rampages being the only evidence of his existence. His crimes include destroying crops, feasting on farm animals and striking fear in the people. At one point, there was even a $100,000 bounty on his head! Make sure to keep yours under control . . . and maybe under wraps with that much being asked for him! From the hooves to the wings, I love everything about this make and hope you do too!

Materials Needed

- 4.0mm crochet hook (G hook)
- 1 (7-oz [198-g]) skein of medium worsted yarn in dark grey (I used Red Heart's Super Saver Charcoal)
- 1 (7-oz [198-g]) skein of medium worsted yarn in black (I used Red Heart's Super Saver Black)
- 1 pair of 9mm safety eyes
- Fiberfill, for stuffing
- Tapestry needle
- Pins, to hold the limbs in place as you sew
- Scissors

Abbreviations

BLO—crochet only in the back loop of the stitch for the following round

ch—chain

dec—invisible decrease

F/o—fasten off

HDC—half double crochet

inc—increase or 2 single crochets in the same stitch

mc—magic circle

sc—single crochet

slpst—slip stitch

Head

In dark grey

Round 1: mc 6. (6)

Round 2: (inc) 6 times. (12)

Round 3: (sc, inc) 6 times. (18)

Round 4: (2 sc, inc) 6 times. (24)

Rounds 5–9: sc around. (24)

Round 10: (3 sc, inc) 6 times. (30)

Rounds 11–16: sc around. (30)

Round 17: (3 sc, dec) 6 times. (24)

Round 18: sc around. (24)

Round 19: (2 sc, dec) 6 times. (18)

Insert the eyes between Rounds 10 and 11 with 11 stitches between them. Stuff the head firmly as you decrease.

Round 20: (sc, dec) 6 times. (12)

Round 21: dec (6)

F/o.

Body

In dark grey

Round 1: mc 6. (6)

Round 2: (inc) 6 times. (12)

Round 3: (sc, inc) 6 times. (18)

Round 4: (2 sc, inc) 6 times. (24)

Round 5: (3 sc, inc) 6 times. (30)

Rounds 6–9: sc around. (30)

Round 10: (3 sc, dec) 6 times. (24)

Round 11: (2 sc, dec) 6 times. (18)

Rounds 12–17: sc around. (18)

Round 18: (sc, dec) 6 times. (12)

F/o, leaving a long tail for sewing.

(continued)

JERSEY DEVIL (CONTINUED)

Thighs—Make 2

In dark grey

Round 1: mc 6. (6)

Round 2: (inc) 6 times. (12)

Rounds 3–10: sc around. (12)

Round 11: (dec) 6 times. (6)

F/o, leaving a long tail for sewing.

Legs—Make 2

In black

Round 1: mc 6. (6)

Round 2: (sc, inc) 3 times. (9)

Round 3: BLO sc around. (9)

Round 4: sc around. (9)

Change to dark grey

Rounds 5–11: sc around. (9)

Round 12: (sc, dec) 3 times. (6)

F/o, leaving a long tail for sewing.

Arms—Make 2

In black

Round 1: mc 6. (6)

Round 2: (sc, inc) 3 times. (9)

Round 3: BLO sc around. (9)

Round 4: sc around. (9)

Change to dark grey

Rounds 5–13: sc around. (9)

F/o, leaving a long tail for sewing.

Tail

In dark grey

Round 1: mc 6. (6)

Rounds 2–15: sc around. (6)

F/o, leaving a long tail for sewing.

Tail Spike

In black

Round 1: mc 5. (5)

Round 2: inc, 4 sc. (6)

Round 3: inc, 5 sc. (7)

Round 4: inc, 6 sc. (8)

Round 5: inc, 7 sc. (9)

F/o, leaving a long tail for sewing.

Horns—Make 2

In black

Round 1: mc 6. (6)

Round 2: (2 sc, inc) 2 times. (8)

Rounds 3–6: sc around. (8)

F/o, leaving a long tail for sewing.

Ears—Make 2

In dark grey

Round 1: ch 4 and turn, in the second chain from hook: slpst, in the next chain: sc, in the last chain: HDC.

F/o, leaving a long tail for sewing.

Wings—Make 2

The wings are made in rows, not rounds. Please read the pattern carefully.

In black

Row 1: ch 5, turn.

Row 2: Start in the second chain from hook, 4 sc, ch 4 and turn.

Row 3: Start in the second chain from hook, 7 sc, ch 1 and turn.

Row 4: Start in the second chain from hook, 4 sc, ch 4 and turn.

Row 5: Start in the second chain from hook, 7 sc, ch 3 and turn.

Row 6: Start in the second chain from hook, 6 sc, ch 4 and turn.

Row 7: Start in the second chain from hook, 9 sc, do not chain or turn.

Row 8: sc around the top of the wing (you will be creating evenly spaced stitches along this ridge).

F/o, leaving a long tail for sewing.

Assembly

Whipstitch the head closed, then stuff the body firmly and attach it to the bottom of the head. Stuff the thighs firmly and attach them to either side of the bottom of the body. Next, lightly stuff the legs and attach them at a slight angle to the bottom of the thighs. Attach the arms to either side of the upper torso (no need to stuff them). Attach the wings to the back and the horns (lightly stuffed) and ears to the top of the head. Lastly, attach the tail to the back of the body, and the tail spike to the very end of it. Use the scissors to cut any leftover yarn tails from the limbs you've attached—now your Jersey Devil is done!

Chapter 5

MISCHIEF MAKERS

A pesky Fairy (page 113), tricky Goblins (page 121) and a science experiment that has gone very, very wrong (page 127) ... this chapter is full of everything nettlesome! Be it throughout history, in the dark of night or in the deep of space, we will be creating a variety of some of the greatest tricksters known to mankind. Get your crochet hook ready and prepare yourself. With these quick and easy patterns, you will soon be surrounded by all of the things that make people uneasy!

MEDUSA

A beautiful woman of tragic origins turned monster and villainized throughout history; hair of snakes, serpent's body, a gaze that will turn the bravest of men to stone . . . sound familiar? It's Medusa! In the following pattern, you will be able to crochet your very own Medusa doll. When designing this pattern, I wanted to capture a softer side of the described hideous monster from Greek mythology. I hope you find her as cute as I do! All those adorable little hair snakes? Oh my gosh! But be careful when casting glances her way; after all the work you put in to making her, I would hate for you to be turned to stone!

Head

In light green

Round 1: mc 6. (6)

Round 2: (inc) 6 times. (12)

Round 3: (sc, inc) 6 times. (18)

Round 4: (2 sc, inc) 6 times. (24)

Round 5: (3 sc, inc) 6 times. (30)

Round 6: (4 sc, inc) 6 times. (36)

Rounds 7–15: sc around. (36)

Insert the 9mm eyes between Rounds 11 and 12 with 6 stitches in between. Start stuffing the head as you decrease.

Round 16: (4 sc, dec) 6 times. (30)

Round 17: (3 sc, dec) 6 times. (24)

Round 18: (2 sc, dec) 6 times. (18)

Round 19: (sc, dec) 6 times. (12)

Round 20: (dec) 6 times. (6)

F/o.

Wig Cap

In dark green

Round 1: mc 6. (6)

Round 2: (inc) 6 times. (12)

Round 3: (sc, inc) 6 times. (18)

Round 4: (2 sc, inc) 6 times. (24)

Round 5: (3 sc, inc) 6 times. (30)

Round 6: (4 sc, inc) 6 times. (36)

Rounds 7–11: sc around. (36)

F/o, leaving a long tail for sewing.

(continued)

Materials Needed

- 4.0mm crochet hook (G hook)
- 1 (7-oz [198-g]) skein of medium worsted yarn in light green (I used Red Heart's Super Saver Frosty Green)
- 1 (7-oz [198-g]) skein of medium worsted yarn in dark green (I used Caron's Simply Soft Dark Sage)
- 1 (7-oz [198-g]) skein of medium worsted yarn in medium green (I used Red Heart's Super Saver Light Sage)
- 1 (7-oz [198-g]) skein of medium worsted yarn in white (I used Big Twist's Value White)
- 1 (7-oz [198-g]) skein of medium worsted yarn in brown (I used Crafter's Secret's Big Idea Brown)
- 1 pair of 9mm safety eyes
- 9 pairs of 6mm safety eyes
- Fiberfill, for stuffing
- Tapestry needle
- Pins, to hold the limbs in place as you sew
- Scissors
- 5 (12-inch [30-cm]) crafting pipe cleaners

Abbreviations

dec–invisible decrease

F/o–fasten off

inc–increase or 2 single crochets in the same stitch

mc–magic circle

sc–single crochet

MEDUSA (CONTINUED)

Snakes—Make 9

In dark green

Round 1: mc 6. (6)

Round 2: (inc) 6 times. (12)

Rounds 3–5: sc around. (12)

Insert a pair of 6mm eyes between Rounds 3 and 4 with 5 stitches in between.

Round 6: (2 sc, dec) 3 times. (9)

Round 7: (sc, dec) 3 times. (6)

There is no need to stuff the snakes. Cut your 5 pipe cleaners into 10 pieces, each about 4 inches (10 cm) long; you only need 9 pieces for this project. Insert a pipe cleaner into the snake's head and continue crocheting around it as you finish the snake. With my tension, I end up with 20 to 22 rounds. You may have more or less depending on how tightly you crochet and what type of yarn you're using. When you reach the end of the pipe cleaner, F/o your yarn and leave a long tail for sewing the snake to her head.

Body

In medium green

Round 1: mc 4. (4)

Round 2: sc around. (4)

Round 3: (sc, inc) 2 times. (6)

Rounds 4–5: sc around. (6)

Round 6: (2 sc, inc) 2 times. (8)

Round 7: sc around. (8)

Round 8: (3 sc, inc) 2 times. (10)

Round 9: sc around. (10)

Round 10: (4 sc, inc) 2 times. (12)

Round 11: sc around. (12)

Round 12: (3 sc, inc) 3 times. (15)

Rounds 13–14: sc around. (15)

Round 15: (4 sc, inc) 3 times. (18)

Rounds 16–17: sc around. (18)

Round 18: (5 sc, inc) 3 times. (21)

Rounds 19–20: sc around. (21)

Change to light green

Round 21: (5 sc, dec) 3 times. (18)

Rounds 22–23: sc around. (18)

Round 24: (4 sc, dec) 3 times. (15)

Change to white

Rounds 25–26: sc around. (15)

Change to light green

Round 27: (3 sc, dec) 3 times. (12)

Round 28: sc around. (12)

F/o, leaving a long tail for sewing.

Then, one by one, remove them from the head, and set them aside carefully. This will help you remember their attachment order and their positioning on the head. Please reference the pictures to see how I laid them, but you can style her "hair" in any way you see fit. Carefully sew each snake onto the head, making sure that as you sew they are lining up the way you envisioned. Once they're all attached, you can re-bend them to make them stand up nicely in their new permanent place.

Next, stuff the thickest portion of the body; do not worry about getting stuffing all the way to the bottom of the tail—that part should stay fairly empty, so it can be easily manipulated to make a slight curl. Once you are content with the firmness, attach the body to the head, then pin the arms and sew them on. The shoulders should be attached right under the head, in line with where you joined the body, which formed the neck of the doll. Use the scissors to cut any leftover yarn tails from all the limbs you've attached. Now your Medusa is done!

Arms—Make 2

In light green

Round 1: mc 6. (6)

Round 2: (sc, inc) 3 times. (9)

Round 3: sc around. (9)

Change to brown

Round 4: (sc, dec) 3 times. (6)

Rounds 5–6: sc around. (6)

Change to light green

Rounds 7–10: sc around. (6)

F/o, leaving a long tail for sewing.

Assembly

First, whipstitch the head closed. Next, attach the wig cap. Make sure you sew it on very securely, as it will be holding a lot of weight!

Next, we'll work on the snakes. Pin each snake onto the head to figure out how you want them to lay. Then, pose them by bending them in the directions you want them to face. They will hold this shape, for the most part, due to the pipe cleaners inside.

FAIRY

Fairies, just like humans, can have all sorts of personalities. Some are benevolent and kind, others are cruel, but the majority are just harmless tricksters. They get a kick out of messing with us mortals! Keep that in mind as you whip up your Fairy and your things start to go missing or you find hair tied in knots or pets annoyed with something trying to ride them! One of my favorite things when making dolls is incorporating "mixed media" crochet, which are added details that are not made of yarn. In this pattern, you will find that I made the wings out of felt. This allows us to cut them in any shape we would like, not to mention finishing them in a fraction of the time it would have taken us to crochet all those stitches in intricate patterns to get a similar result.

Head

In preferred skin tone

Round 1: mc 6. (6)

Round 2: (inc) 6 times. (12)

Round 3: (sc, inc) 6 times. (18)

Round 4: (2 sc, inc) 6 times. (24)

Round 5: (3 sc, inc) 6 times. (30)

Round 6: (4 sc, inc) 6 times. (36)

Rounds 7–15: sc around. (36)

Insert the eyes between Rounds 11 and 12 with 6 stitches in between. Start stuffing the head as you decrease.

Round 16: (4 sc, dec) 6 times. (30)

Round 17: (3 sc, dec) 6 times. (24)

Round 18: (2 sc, dec) 6 times. (18)

Round 19: (sc, dec) 6 times. (12)

Round 20: (dec) 6 times. (6)

F/o.

Wig Cap

In pink

Round 1: mc 6. (6)

Round 2: (inc) 6 times. (12)

Round 3: (sc, inc) 6 times. (18)

Round 4: (2 sc, inc) 6 times. (24)

Round 5: (3 sc, inc) 6 times. (30)

Round 6: (4 sc, inc) 6 times. (36)

Rounds 7–11: sc around. (36)

F/o, leaving a long tail for sewing.

Hair

Sew the wig cap to the top of the head. Leave any excess yarn from sewing attached; we will use it to attach the strands of hair. If it is not long enough (you will need about 10 inches [25 cm]), then cut a new strand of yarn and use it instead. Weave the strand of yarn to the front of the wig cap; this is where we will begin attaching our hair.

(continued)

Materials Needed

- 4.0mm crochet hook (G hook)
- 2.75mm crochet hook (C hook)
- 1 (7-oz [198-g]) skein of medium worsted yarn in preferred skin tone (I used Red Heart's Super Saver Buff)
- 1 (7-oz [198-g]) skein of medium worsted yarn in pink (I used Caron's Simply Soft Watermelon)
- 1 pair of 9mm safety eyes
- Fiberfill, for stuffing
- Tapestry needle
- Pins, to hold the limbs in place as you sew
- Scissors
- Fabri-Tac glue or hot glue
- 1 sheet of white felt

Abbreviations

dec–invisible decrease

F/o–fasten off

inc–increase or 2 single crochets in the same stitch

mc–magic circle

sc–single crochet

FAIRY (CONTINUED)

Next cut about 40 strands of pink yarn, about 8 inches (20 cm) long. Begin sewing bundles of them to the wig cap; I find 4 strands is a perfect thickness for each section. Keep your sewing line straight, as this will be where the hair parts. Pull your sewing strand very tight every time you secure a hair bundle, and maintain that same tightness as you continue down the wig cap. I usually stop attaching bundles of hair once I get to the back of the head where attaching the hair would become a vertical task. The last step is to apply a very thin line of glue on each side of the part to make sure the hair doesn't easily come out of the sewn part we just created. Remember: A little bit of glue goes a very long way. Set the head aside somewhere safe until the glue has dried. Leave the hair strands long for now.

Body

Starting with the first leg, in pink

Round 1: mc 6. (6)

Round 2: (inc) 6 times. (12)

Round 3: sc around. (12)

Change to preferred skin tone

Rounds 4–6: sc around. (12)

Change to pink

Round 7: sc around. (12)

F/o.

Second leg, in pink

Round 1: mc 6. (6)

Round 2: (inc) 6 times. (12)

Round 3: sc around. (12)

Change to preferred skin tone

Rounds 4–6: sc around. (12)

Change to pink

Round 7: sc around. (12)

Do not fasten off; join the next stitch into the first leg, and consider this the first stitch of Round 8.

Round 8: sc around. (24)

Rounds 9–15: sc around. (24)

Round 16: (2 sc, dec) 6 times. (18)

Round 17: sc around. (18)

Round 18: (sc, dec) 6 times. (12)

F/o, leaving a long tail for sewing.

Arms—Make 2

In preferred skin tone

Round 1: mc 6. (6)

Rounds 2–8: sc around. (6)

F/o, leaving a long tail for sewing.

Once the glue from the hair has dried, whipstitch the bottom of the head closed. Stuff the body firmly, and attach it to the bottom of the head.

Gown

In pink

Now we will be crocheting the length of the gown.

Round 1: Flip your doll around so the back is facing you, then turn it upside down (so the feet are now at the top). Insert your C hook in the middle of the back between Rounds 10 and 11, yarn over with pink yarn and then pull it through the stitch, tightening down. You are going to continue to crochet around the body with single crochet stitches. Since we crochet in the round when we make our dolls, there is a natural spiral to the stitches. This means you will not end up connecting back to the original stitch but either above or below it, depending on how you're looking at it. Since this is the case, you will need to "jump" a round to get back in line with where you started. I recommend doing this jump only right before you get to the final stitch and in the back of the doll. This will appear a little off if you look super closely, which is why I like to hide it on the doll's back. You should have about 24 stitches when you get back to where you started.

Rounds 2–5: sc around. (~24)

F/o, and weave in tail.

Assembly

Sew the arms to either side of the body (no need to stuff them). Use the scissors to cut any leftover yarn tails. Now, here is some room for creativity! Cut 2 fairy-shaped wings out of felt; you can make them as simple or elaborate as you'd like and in any color, shape or size. When you are happy with your wings, glue them to the back of your Fairy, and trim her hair. She is finished!

KRAMPUS

We tell children to behave during Christmastime because "Santa is watching . . ." in a fun, singsong tone, insinuating that if they misbehave, they may not get the presents that they have their hearts set on. In Central Europe, they have a little bit bigger of a motivator. Krampus is a half-goat, half-demon creature who punishes children who misbehave during Christmastime by beating them with branches, or, in extreme cases, by taking them! Crochet your own Krampus as a fun joke . . . or use it as a reminder for those children who need some extra motivation throughout the later part of the year . . . kidding, kidding! But please do enjoy this crochet pattern; there have been many movies and stories about Krampus and any super-fan would love him. Plus, who could resist those little hooves?

Materials Needed

- 4.0mm crochet hook (G hook)
- 1 (7-oz [198-g]) skein of medium worsted yarn in black (I used Red Heart's Super Saver Black)
- 1 (7-oz [198-g]) skein of medium worsted yarn in grey (I used Caron's Simply Soft Grey Heather)
- 1 (7-oz [198-g]) skein of medium worsted yarn in red (I used I Love This Yarn's Red)
- 1 pair of 9mm safety eyes
- Fiberfill, for stuffing
- Tapestry needle
- Pins, to hold the limbs in place as you sew
- Scissors

Abbreviations

BLO—crochet only in the back loop of the stitch for the following round

ch—chain

dec—invisible decrease

F/o—fasten off

HDC—half double crochet

inc—increase or 2 single crochets in the same stitch

mc—magic circle

sc—single crochet

slpst—slip stitch

Head

In black

Round 1: mc 6. (6)

Round 2: (inc) 6 times. (12)

Round 3: (sc, inc) 6 times. (18)

Round 4: (2 sc, inc) 6 times. (24)

Round 5: (3 sc, inc) 6 times. (30)

Rounds 6–10: sc around. (30)

Round 11: (4 sc, inc) 6 times. (36)

Rounds 12–14: sc around. (36)

Place the eyes between Rounds 11 and 12 with 6 stitches in between. Stuff the head firmly as you decrease.

Round 15: (4 sc, dec) 6 times. (30)

Round 16: (3 sc, dec) 6 times. (24)

Round 17: (2 sc, dec) 6 times. (18)

Round 18: (sc, dec) 6 times. (12)

Round 19: (dec) 6 times. (6)

F/o.

Muzzle

In black

Round 1: mc 6. (6)

Round 2: (inc) 6 times. (12)

Round 3: (3 sc, inc) 3 times. (15)

Rounds 4–5: sc around. (15)

F/o, leaving a long tail for sewing.

Body

In black

Round 1: mc 6. (6)

Round 2: (inc) 6 times. (12)

Round 3: (sc, inc) 6 times. (18)

Round 4: (2 sc, inc) 6 times. (24)

Round 5: (3 sc, inc) 6 times. (30)

Rounds 6–9: sc around. (30)

Round 10: (3 sc, dec) 6 times. (24)

Round 11: (2 sc, dec) 6 times. (18)

(continued)

KRAMPUS (CONTINUED)

Rounds 12–17: sc around. (18)

Round 18: (sc, dec) 6 times. (12)

F/o, leaving a long tail for sewing.

Thighs–Make 2

In black

Round 1: mc 6. (6)

Round 2: (inc) 6 times. (12)

Rounds 3–10: sc around. (12)

Round 11: (dec) 6 times. (6)

F/o, leaving a long tail for sewing.

Legs–Make 2

In black

Round 1: mc 6. (6)

Round 2: (sc, inc) 3 times. (9)

Round 3: BLO sc around. (9)

Rounds 4–11: sc around. (9)

Round 12: (sc, dec) 3 times. (6)

F/o, leaving a long tail for sewing.

Arms–Make 2

In black

Round 1: mc 6. (6)

Round 2: (sc, inc) 3 times. (9)

Round 3: BLO sc around. (9)

Rounds 4–13: sc around. (9)

F/o, leaving a long tail for sewing.

Tail

In black

Round 1: mc 6. (6)

Rounds 2–11: sc around. (6)

F/o, leaving a long tail for sewing.

Horns–Make 2

In grey

Round 1: mc 6. (6)

Round 2: (2 sc, inc) 2 times. (8)

Rounds 3–6: sc around. (8)

F/o, leaving a long tail for sewing.

Ears–Make 2

In black

Round 1: ch 4 and turn, in the second chain from hook: slpst, in the next chain: sc, in the last chain: HDC.

F/o, leaving a long tail for sewing.

Tongue

In red

Round 1: ch 14 and turn, slpst in each chain, starting from the second chain from the hook. (13)

F/o, leaving a long tail for sewing.

Assembly

Whipstitch the head closed, then stuff the body firmly and attach it to the bottom of the head. Stuff the thighs firmly and attach them to either side of the bottom of the body. Next, lightly stuff the legs and attach them at a slight angle to the bottom of the thighs. Attach the arms to either side of the upper torso (no need to stuff them).

Pin the muzzle to the front of the face, in between the eyes. Start sewing it on, but stop when it is about 75 percent attached. Stuff the muzzle to your desired firmness, then finish sewing it on. Attach the horns to the top of the head and the ears to either side, slightly in front of the them.

Attach the tail to the bottom of the back. Make the tail a tuft of hair using 3 strands of grey yarn, about 6 inches (15 cm) long. Attach them to the end of the tail using the latch hook method.

Finally, use a strand of grey yarn to embroider a nose to the top of the muzzle, and sew the tongue to the bottom of the muzzle. Use the scissors to cut any leftover yarn tails. Your Krampus is now done and ready to make sure children are behaving for their parents!

KITSUNE

Kitsune originate from Japanese mythology. They are clever and tricky foxes that possess special abilities. The number of tails a Kitsune has can tell you a lot about them, and they can have up to nine! As they age, and grow wiser, they not only grow more powerful, but they grow additional tails. It can take them up to 100 years to grow just one tail. So, if you ever run into a nine-tailed fox, it may be best to just turn the other way! Keep that in mind when deciding how many tails to make for your Kitsune. Just like everything, there are good and bad Kitsune. So don't worry when making yours, I'm sure you can nurture it to be as you wish! But be warned, even a good Kitsune may enjoy some mischief every once in a while. . . .

Materials Needed

- 4.0mm crochet hook (G hook)
- 1 (7-oz [198-g]) skein of medium worsted yarn in white (I used Red Heart's Super Saver White)
- 1 pair of 12mm safety eyes
- Fiberfill, for stuffing
- Tapestry needle
- Pins, to hold the limbs in place as you sew
- Scissors
- Scrap piece of black yarn, for embroidering the nose

Abbreviations

dec–invisible decrease
F/o–fasten off
inc–increase or 2 single crochets in the same stitch
mc–magic circle
sc–single crochet

Head

Round 1: mc 6. (6)

Round 2: (inc) 6 times. (12)

Round 3: (sc, inc) 6 times. (18)

Round 4: (2 sc, inc) 6 times. (24)

Round 5: (3 sc, inc) 6 times. (30)

Round 6: (4 sc, inc) 6 times. (36)

Rounds 7–12: sc around. (36)

Round 13: (5 sc, inc) 6 times. (42)

Rounds 14–16: sc around. (42)

Insert the eyes between Rounds 12 and 13 with 7 stitches between them. Stuff the head firmly as you decrease.

Round 17: (5 sc, dec) 6 times. (36)

Round 18: (4 sc, dec) 6 times. (30)

Round 19: (3 sc, dec) 6 times. (24)

Round 20: (2 sc, dec) 6 times. (18)

Round 21: (sc, dec) 6 times. (12)

Round 22: (dec) 6 times. (6)

F/o.

Body

Round 1: mc 6. (6)

Round 2: (inc) 6 times. (12)

Round 3: (sc, inc) 6 times. (18)

Round 4: (2 sc, inc) 6 times. (24)

Round 5: (3 sc, inc) 6 times. (30)

Round 6: (4 sc, inc) 6 times. (36)

Rounds 7–9: sc around. (36)

Round 10: (4 sc, dec) 6 times. (30)

Round 11: sc around. (30)

Round 12: (3 sc, dec) 6 times. (24)

Rounds 13–15: sc around. (24)

Round 16: (2 sc, dec) 6 times. (18)

Round 17: sc around. (18)

F/o, leaving a long tail for sewing.

(continued)

KITSUNE (CONTINUED)

Haunches—Make 2

Round 1: mc 6. (6)

Round 2: (inc) 6 times. (12)

Round 3: (3 sc, inc) 3 times. (15)

Round 4: sc around. (15)

F/o, leaving a long tail for sewing.

Back Paws—Make 2

Round 1: mc 6. (6)

Round 2: (2 sc, inc) 2 times. (8)

Round 3: sc around. (8)

F/o, leaving a long tail for sewing.

Front Legs—Make 2

Round 1: mc 6. (6)

Round 2: (2 sc, inc) 2 times. (8)

Rounds 3–13: sc around. (8)

F/o, leaving a long tail for sewing.

Muzzle

Round 1: mc 6. (6)

Round 2: (sc, inc) 3 times. (9)

Round 3: (2 sc, inc) 3 times. (12)

Round 4: (3 sc, inc) 3 times. (15)

Round 5: sc around. (15)

Round 6: (4 sc, inc) 3 times. (18)

Rounds 7–8: sc around. (18)

F/o, leaving a long tail for sewing.

Ears—Make 2

Round 1: mc 4. (4)

Round 2: (sc, inc) 2 times. (6)

Round 3: (2 sc, inc) 2 times. (8)

Round 4: (3 sc, inc) 2 times. (10)

Round 5: (4 sc, inc) 2 times. (12)

Rounds 6–9: sc around. (12)

F/o, leaving a long tail for sewing.

Tails

Make as many as you'd like! Kitsune typically have between 2 to 9 tails, depending on their age. I made 7 for mine.

Round 1: mc 6. (6)

Round 2: (2 sc, inc) 2 times. (8)

Round 3: (3 sc, inc) 2 times. (10)

Round 4: (4 sc, inc) 2 times. (12)

Rounds 5–12: sc around. (12)

Round 13: (dec) 6 times. (6)

F/o, leaving a long tail for sewing.

Assembly

Whipstitch the head closed, then stuff the body firmly and attach it to the bottom of the head. Start sewing the haunches to either side of the body, but before completely attaching them, stuff them to your desired firmness. Then finish them off. Next, attach the back paws to the front of the haunches, checking the balance of your doll as you sew them to make sure they are helping keep your Kitsune upright. Next attach the front legs to the front of the torso (no need to stuff them).

Attach the ears to the top of the head and the muzzle to the middle of the face (in between the eyes). Use the scrap of black yarn and embroider a nose to the top of the muzzle.

Stuff all of the tails and pin them to the back of your doll to decide on your preferred placement. Once you're happy, sew them all on. Use the scissors to cut any leftover yarn tails. Your Kitsune is now finished!

GOBLIN

Goblins are little mischievous creatures who are known for their greed. They love stealing gold and jewelry and have some magic abilities up their sleeves, so be very cautious when making them! But this pattern is just for a baby goblin, with big ol' eyes and ears; he looks so sweet and innocent . . . how much trouble could he get into? Are these my famous last words?

Materials Needed

- 4.0mm crochet hook (G hook)
- 1 (7-oz [198-g]) skein of medium worsted yarn in dark green (I used I Love This Yarn's Forest Green)
- 1 pair of 12mm safety eyes
- Fiberfill, for stuffing
- Tapestry needle
- Pins, to hold the limbs in place as you sew
- Scissors
- 1 sheet of white felt

Abbreviations

dec–invisible decrease

F/o–fasten off

inc–increase or 2 single crochets in the same stitch

mc–magic circle

sc–single crochet

Head

Round 1: mc 6. (6)

Round 2: (inc) 6 times. (12)

Round 3: (sc, inc) 6 times. (18)

Round 4: (2 sc, inc) 6 times. (24)

Round 5: (3 sc, inc) 6 times. (30)

Round 6: (4 sc, inc) 6 times. (36)

Rounds 7–12: sc around. (36)

Round 13: (5 sc, inc) 6 times. (42)

Rounds 14–17: sc around. (42)

Pause crocheting here and cut 2 circles out of white felt, approximately ½ inch (1.3 cm) in diameter. Cut a slit in the middle and insert an eye post into each circle, making the white circle the background of the eye. Trim your circle down so the top is thinner (I make mine nearly invisible) and the bottom is wider. This will give your plush an adorable "looking up" expression. When you're happy with your trimming, insert the eyes between Rounds 13 and 14 with 7 stitches in between them. Stuff the head firmly as you decrease.

Round 18: (5 sc, dec) 6 times. (36)

Round 19: (4 sc, dec) 6 times. (30)

Round 20: (3 sc, dec) 6 times. (24)

Round 21: (2 sc, dec) 6 times. (18)

Round 22: (sc, dec) 6 times. (12)

Round 23: (dec) 6 times. (6)

F/o.

Body

Round 1: mc 6. (6)

Round 2: (inc) 6 times. (12)

Round 3: (sc, inc) 6 times. (18)

Round 4: (2 sc, inc) 6 times. (24)

Round 5: (3 sc, inc) 6 times. (30)

Round 6: (4 sc, inc) 6 times. (36)

Rounds 7–10: sc around. (36)

Round 11: (4 sc, dec) 6 times. (30)

Rounds 12–15: sc around. (30)

Round 16: (3 sc, dec) 6 times. (24)

Round 17: (2 sc, dec) 6 times. (18)

Round 18: (sc, dec) 6 times. (12)

F/o, leaving a long tail for sewing.

(continued)

GOBLIN (CONTINUED)

Legs—Make 2
Round 1: mc 6. (6)

Round 2: (inc) 6 times. (12)

Round 3: (3 sc, inc) 3 times. (15)

Rounds 4–6: sc around. (15)

Round 7: (3 sc, dec) 3 times. (12)

Rounds 8–10: sc around. (12)

Round 11: (2 sc, dec) 3 times. (9)

Rounds 12–14: sc around. (9)

F/o, leaving a long tail for sewing.

Arms—Make 2
Round 1: mc 6. (6)

Round 2: (inc) 6 times. (12)

Rounds 3–7: sc around. (12)

Round 8: (2 sc, dec) 3 times. (9)

Rounds 9–13: sc around. (9)

F/o, leaving a long tail for sewing.

Ears—Make 2
Round 1: mc 6. (6)

Round 2: sc around. (6)

Round 3: (2 sc, inc) 2 times. (8)

Round 4: (3 sc, inc) 2 times. (10)

Round 5: (4 sc, inc) 2 times. (12)

Rounds 6–9: sc around. (12)

Round 10: (4 sc, dec) 2 times. (10)

F/o, leaving a long tail for sewing.

Assembly
Whipstitch the head closed, then stuff the body firmly and attach it to the bottom of the head. Stuff the legs and sew them onto the bottom of the body; I chose to make my Goblin in a sitting position, but you can pose and attach yours in any way you want! Lightly stuff the arms and attach them to either side of the upper body. Pin the ears to either side of the head, and make sure they are in line with one another before sewing them on. Once you have those secure, use the scissors to cut any leftover yarn tails from the limbs you've attached and your Goblin is finished!

BOOGIE MAN

The Boogie Man is a terrifying creature that has been plaguing children's nightmares since the beginning of time. He lurks in the shadows, hides under beds and can just magically disappear when concerned parents come to oust him . . . and then reappear as soon as the door closes behind them! After you make yours, you may have a hard time finding him if you let him out of your sight, so be warned! This pattern includes the long creepy fingers that children have claimed to see stretching out from under their bed, and a menacing sharp-teeth-filled smile.

Materials Needed

- 4.0mm crochet hook (G hook)
- 1 (7-oz [198-g]) skein of medium worsted yarn in black (I used Caron's One Pound Black)
- Fiberfill, for stuffing
- Tapestry needle
- Pins, to hold the limbs in place as you sew
- Scissors
- 1 sheet of white felt
- Fabri-Tac glue or hot glue

Abbreviations

ch–chain

dec–invisible decrease

F/o–fasten off

inc–increase or 2 single crochets in the same stitch

mc–magic circle

sc–single crochet

slpst–slip stitch

Head

Round 1: mc 6. (6)

Round 2: (inc) 6 times. (12)

Round 3: (sc, inc) 6 times. (18)

Round 4: (2 sc, inc) 6 times. (24)

Round 5: (3 sc, inc) 6 times. (30)

Round 6: (4 sc, inc) 6 times. (36)

Rounds 7–15: sc around. (36)

Round 16: (4 sc, dec) 6 times. (30)

Round 17: (3 sc, dec) 6 times. (24)

Stuff firmly as you continue to decrease.

Round 18: (2 sc, dec) 6 times. (18)

Round 19: (sc, dec) 6 times. (12)

Round 20: (dec) 6 times. (6)

F/o.

Body

Round 1: mc 6. (6)

Round 2: (inc) 6 times. (12)

Round 3: (sc, inc) 6 times. (18)

Round 4: (2 sc, inc) 6 times. (24)

Round 5: (3 sc, inc) 6 times. (30)

Rounds 6–8: sc around. (30)

Round 9: (3 sc, dec) 6 times. (24)

Rounds 10–12: sc around. (24)

Round 13: (2 sc, dec) 6 times. (18)

Rounds 14–16: sc around. (18)

F/o leaving a long tail for sewing.

Thighs–Make 2

Round 1: mc 6. (6)

Round 2: (sc, inc) 3 times. (9)

Rounds 3–7: sc around. (9)

F/o, leaving a long tail for sewing.

(continued)

BOOGIE MAN (CONTINUED)

Legs–Make 2

Round 1: mc 6. (6)

Rounds 2–8: sc around. (6)

F/o, leaving a long tail for sewing.

Arms–Make 2

Round 1: mc 6. (6)

Rounds 2–9: sc around. (6)

F/o, leaving a long tail for sewing.

Fingers–Make 6

Ch 6 and turn, in the second chain from hook slpst, continue to slpst in the remaining chains. (5)

F/o, leaving a long tail for sewing.

Assembly

Whipstitch the head closed, then stuff the body firmly and attach it to the lower back of the head. (I realize there are no distinguishing features on the head, but the side that the body is *not* attached to is now the front of the head.) Stuff the thighs and attach them to either side of the back of the body. Be careful with your sewing here. We want our Boogie Man to be in a crouching position; when I attached the thighs to my doll,

I made sure they were not only angled downward, but also slightly forward facing (just like our thighs would be if we crouched down in this position).

Next, attach the legs to the bottom of the thighs right under where the knees would be (no need to stuff them). Then attach the arms to either side of where the body and head are joined (no need to stuff them). Again, take angling into consideration as you sew them on. I positioned mine so they would slightly prop up my body. The goal is to make

this Boogie Man look like he is crouched under a bed! Attach 3 fingers to each hand. Use the scissors to cut any leftover yarn tails from the limbs you've attached.

Finally, cut little triangles about ½ inch (1.3 cm) long out of white felt and glue them to the front of the head where the face would be. I cut 9 of them and staggered them, slightly spaced. But you can add as many teeth as you would like. Once your glue is dry, your Boogie Man is ready to go!

FRANKENSTEIN'S MONSTER

Everyone knows the tale of Dr. Frankenstein—a mad scientist who creates a lifeform and then flees from it out of fear. He abandoned a confused and lost creature who has feelings, you know! The creature yearns to belong, but due to his grotesque appearance and origins, he is rejected at every turn . . . until finally he snaps . . . then they have the nerve to call *him* the monster? Meet my very sweet rendition of this classical creature. He is good-natured and pure, and with a little love I'm sure he will do well in our world. But he is a little sensitive . . . so tread lightly!

Head

In green

Round 1: mc 6. (6)

Round 2: (inc) 6 times. (12)

Round 3: (sc, inc) 6 times. (18)

Round 4: (2 sc, inc) 6 times. (24)

Round 5: (3 sc, inc) 6 times. (30)

Round 6: (4 sc, inc) 6 times. (36)

Rounds 7–15: sc around. (36)

Round 16: (4 sc, dec) 6 times. (30)

Round 17: (3 sc, dec) 6 times. (24)

Insert the eyes between Rounds 11 and 12 with 6 stitches in between. Stuff firmly as you continue to decrease.

Round 18: (2 sc, dec) 6 times. (18)

Round 19: (sc, dec) 6 times. (12)

Round 20: (dec) 6 times. (6)

F/o.

Wig Cap

In black

Round 1: mc 6. (6)

Round 2: (inc) 6 times. (12)

Round 3: (sc, inc) 6 times. (18)

Round 4: (2 sc, inc) 6 times. (24)

Round 5: (3 sc, inc) 6 times. (30)

Round 6: (4 sc, inc) 6 times. (36)

Rounds 7–11: sc around. (36)

F/o, leaving a long tail for sewing.

Ears—Make 2

In green

Round 1: mc 5. (5)

Smoosh all stitches to one side of the magic circle to create a semi-circle.

F/o, leaving a long tail for sewing.

(continued)

Materials Needed

- 4.0mm crochet hook (G hook)
- 1 (7-oz [198-g]) skein of medium worsted yarn in green (I used I Love This Yarn's Mid Green)
- 1 (7-oz [198-g]) skein of medium worsted yarn in black (I used Big Twist's Value Black)
- 1 (7-oz [198-g]) skein of medium worsted yarn in brown (I used Big Twist's Value Chocolate)
- 1 (7-oz [198-g]) skein of medium worsted yarn in grey (I used I Love This Yarn's Graymist)
- 1 pair of 9mm safety eyes
- Fiberfill, for stuffing
- Tapestry needle
- Pins, to hold the limbs in place as you sew
- Scissors
- 10-inch (25-cm) strand black embroidery thread

Abbreviations

dec—invisible decrease

F/o—fasten off

inc—increase or 2 single crochets in the same stitch

mc—magic circle

sc—single crochet

FRANKEN-STEIN'S MONSTER (CONTINUED)

Arms—Make 2

In green

Round 1: mc 6. (6)

Round 2: (sc, inc) 3 times. (9)

Rounds 3–4: sc around. (9)

Change to brown

Rounds 5–9: sc around. (9)

F/o, leaving a long tail for sewing.

Body

Starting with the first leg, in green

Round 1: mc 6. (6)

Round 2: (inc) 6 times. (12)

Rounds 3–4: sc around. (12)

Change to black

Rounds 5–7: sc around. (12)

F/o.

Second leg, in green

Round 1: mc 6. (6)

Round 2: (inc) 6 times. (12)

Rounds 3–4: sc around. (12)

Change to black

Rounds 5–7: sc around. (12)

Do not fasten off; join the next stitch into the first leg, and consider this the first stitch of Round 8.

Rounds 8–10: sc around. (24)

Change to brown

Rounds 11–15: sc around. (24)

Round 16: (2 sc, dec) 6 times. (18)

Round 17: sc around. (18)

Round 18: (sc, dec) 6 times. (12)

F/o, leaving a long tail for sewing.

Bolts—Make 2

In grey

Round 1: mc 6. (6)

Rounds 2–3: sc around. (6)

F/o, leaving a long tail for sewing.

Assembly

First, whipstitch the head closed and sew the wig cap to the top of the head. I have mine angled so there are about 4 rows visible in between the eyes and the front hairline. Once the wig cap is secure, use the remaining tail—or cut a new strand of black yarn about 10 inches (25 cm) long if there is not enough leftover—and begin embroidering bangs that overlap the edge of the wig cap and the forehead. Please use the finished doll pictured as a reference. (*Tip: Planning where you want your bangs ahead of time using sewing pins can save you a lot of time and frustration!*) Next, sew the ears onto either side of the head, and use some black yarn to embroider sideburns too. This technique of embroidering hair can be challenging at first, but don't give up! The result is always super cute and worth it.

Next, stuff the body firmly and attach it to the bottom of the head. Attach the arms to either side of the body in line with where the head and the body are joined (no need to stuff them). Attach the bolts to the bottom of the head (no need to stuff these). Use the scissors to cut any leftover yarn tails.

Using your black embroidery thread, embroider some stitches on your little creature's face and some eyebrows. Finally, using the green yarn, embroider some exposed "skin" on top of the pants and shirt to give them a tattered clothing look. With this, your creature is finished!

THE GREYS

Have you ever looked up at the stars and wondered if there are other forms of life out there? As soon as you crochet these aliens you will be able to prove there is! A lot of people find aliens creepy and unsettling, but in this chibi style, I think more people than not will agree they can be quite adorable. Get your hook and your yarn, and get ready to make one of the cutest lifeforms out there! These are a great stash-buster; you can make them in any color (despite their name of "The Greys") and they take such a little amount of yarn.

Materials Needed

- 4.0mm crochet hook (G hook)
- 2 (7-oz [198-g]) skeins of medium worsted yarn in grey (I used Caron's One Pound Soft Gray)
- Fiberfill, for stuffing
- Tapestry needle
- Pins, to hold the limbs in place as you sew
- Scissors
- 1 sheet of black felt
- Fabri-Tac glue or hot glue

Abbreviations

dec–invisible decrease
F/o–fasten off
inc–increase or 2 single crochets in the same stitch
mc–magic circle
sc–single crochet

Head

Round 1: mc 6. (6)

Round 2: (inc) 6 times. (12)

Round 3: (sc, inc) 6 times. (18)

Round 4: (2 sc, inc) 6 times. (24)

Round 5: (3 sc, inc) 6 times. (30)

Round 6: (4 sc, inc) 6 times. (36)

Rounds 7–13: sc around. (36)

Round 14: (4 sc, dec) 6 times. (30)

Round 15: sc around. (30)

Round 16: (3 sc, dec) 6 times. (24)

Round 17: sc around. (24)

Stuff firmly as you continue to decrease.

Round 18: (2 sc, dec) 6 times. (18)

Round 19: sc around. (18)

Round 20: (sc, dec) 6 times. (12)

Round 21: (dec) 6 times. (6)

F/o.

Arms–Make 2

Round 1: mc 6. (6)

Round 2: (sc, inc) 3 times. (9)

Rounds 3–9: sc around. (9)

F/o.

Body

Starting with the first leg

Round 1: mc 6. (6)

Round 2: (inc) 6 times. (12)

Rounds 3–7: sc around. (12)

F/o.

(continued)

THE GREYS (CONTINUED)

Second leg

Round 1: mc 6. (6)

Round 2: (inc) 6 times. (12)

Rounds 3–7: sc around. (12)

Do not fasten off; join the next stitch into the first leg, and consider this the first stitch of Round 8.

Round 8: sc around. (24)

Rounds 9–15: sc around. (24)

Round 16: (2 sc, dec) 6 times. (18)

Round 17: sc around. (18)

Round 18: (sc, dec) 6 times. (12)

F/o, leaving a long tail for sewing.

Eyes

Cut 2 oval shapes out of black felt. Mine measured to be 1¼ inches (3 cm) long and ¾ inch (2 cm) wide. You will want to make your eyes proportionate to the head you made. Yours and mine will be slightly different, as no two tensions are the same, and we may be using different yarn. This is totally fine, as you can just cut slightly bigger or smaller ovals depending on your head size.

Alternative color

Assembly

Whipstitch the head closed. Stuff the body firmly and attach it to the bottom of the head. Attach your arms to either side of the torso, right under where the head and body are joined. Next, glue on the eyes. Remember: A little glue goes a long way! If you use too much it can bleed through the felt. I glued my eyes between Rounds 8 and 16, and gave each a slight angle. Now your little alien is done!

SCI-FI ROBOT

Robots, especially in the sci-fi genre, start out as designs to help make life easier for humankind, but something always goes wrong and comes in between the artificial intelligence and their human. Don't worry, that won't be the case here. These robots are programmed to bring joy to anyone who holds them; that's their only function! Whether it's keeping people company as a desk buddy next to their monitor while they work or going on adventures in the hands of a little one, joy abounds! With the following pattern, you will be able to build an army of benevolent androids with which to fill our world. My favorite part about this pattern is how customizable these little ones are. You can do any color combination, and if you choose to paint the safety eyes like I did, you can give them an even more complete look.

Materials Needed

- 4.0mm crochet hook (G hook)
- 1 (7-oz [198-g]) skein of medium worsted yarn in grey (I used Big Twist's Value Soft Gray)
- 1 (7-oz [198-g]) skein of medium worsted yarn in black (I used Big Twist's Value Black)
- 1 pair of 9mm safety eyes (painted as specified on page 13)
- Fiberfill, for stuffing
- Tapestry needle
- Pins, to hold the limbs in place as you sew
- Scissors
- 1 sheet of white felt
- Fabri-Tac glue or hot glue

Abbreviations

BLO—crochet only in the back loop of the stitch for the following round

dec—invisible decrease

F/o—fasten off

inc—increase or 2 single crochets in the same stitch

mc—magic circle

sc—single crochet

Head

In grey

Round 1: mc 6. (6)

Round 2: (inc) 6 times. (12)

Round 3: (sc, inc) 6 times. (18)

Round 4: (2 sc, inc) 6 times. (24)

Round 5: (3 sc, inc) 6 times. (30)

Round 6: (4 sc, inc) 6 times. (36)

Rounds 7–15: sc around. (36)

Insert the eyes between Rounds 11 and 12 with 6 stitches in between. Stuff the head firmly as you continue to decrease.

Round 16: (4 sc, dec) 6 times. (30)

Round 17: (3 sc, dec) 6 times. (24)

Round 18: (2 sc, dec) 6 times. (18)

Round 19: (sc, dec) 6 times. (12)

Round 20: (dec) 6 times. (6)

F/o.

Body

Starting with the first leg, in grey

Round 1: mc 6. (6)

Round 2: (inc) 6 times. (12)

Round 3: (sc, inc) 6 times. (18)

Round 4: BLO sc around. (18)

Rounds 5–7: sc around. (18)

Round 8: (sc, dec) 6 times. (12)

Change to black

Round 9: BLO sc around. (12)

Rounds 10–11: sc around. (12)

F/o.

(continued)

SCI-FI ROBOT (CONTINUED)

Second leg, in grey

Round 1: mc 6. (6)

Round 2: (inc) 6 times. (12)

Round 3: (sc, inc) 6 times. (18)

Round 4: BLO sc around. (18)

Rounds 5–7: sc around. (18)

Round 8: (sc, dec) 6 times. (12)

Change to black

Round 9: BLO sc around. (12)

Rounds 10–11: sc around. (12)

Change to grey

Do not fasten off the second leg; join the next stitch into the first leg, and consider this the first stitch of Round 12.

Round 12: sc around. (24)

Round 13: (2 sc, dec) 6 times. (18)

Round 14: sc around. (18)

Change to black

Round 15: BLO sc around. (18)

Round 16: sc around. (18)

Change to grey

Rounds 17–18: sc around. (18)

Round 19: (sc, dec) 6 times. (12)

Round 20: sc around. (12)

F/o, leaving a long tail for sewing.

Alternative color

Arms—Make 2

In grey

Round 1: mc 6. (6)

Round 2: (inc) 6 times. (12)

Round 3: BLO sc around. (12)

Rounds 4–5: sc around. (12)

Round 6: (2 sc, dec) 3 times. (9)

Change to black

Round 7: BLO sc around. (9)

Rounds 8–9: sc around. (9)

F/o, leaving a long tail for sewing.

Side Bolts—Make 2

In grey

Round 1: mc 6. (6)

Round 2: (inc) 6 times. (12)

F/o, leaving a long tail for sewing.

Assembly

First, whipstitch the head closed. Stuff the body firmly, and attach it to the bottom of the head. Stuff the arms and attach them to the side of the body. Next pin the side bolts to the side of the head and sew them on. Cut 2 felt circles (the same color as the eyes) about ½ inch (1.3 cm) in diameter and glue them to the center of each bolt, then cut a smaller felt circle, about ⅓ inch (8 mm) in diameter, and glue it to the center of the chest. You can decorate your Sci-Fi Robot however you see fit. This is just how I decided to style mine.

Chapter 6

WINGED BEASTS

It's a bird! It's a plane! Wait, no . . . that's a Dragon (page 139)! And that's a Gargoyle (page 157)! I think it's safe to say we have arrived in winged beasts territory. Keep your eyes on the sky while we venture through this one; you don't want to miss any of the six flying creatures I have designed for you. Wings are complicated! In this chapter, we will make several different kinds of wings. If you find you adore one wing style, let's say for the Dragon, but don't find the Phoenix style (page 145) as much fun, you can totally mix and match! Just because I only used the felt-feathered technique on the Phoenix doesn't mean it wouldn't be absolutely breathtaking on the Griffin (page 143). Don't feel restricted to following the pattern exactly; this book is a tool and as we continue to work through it, you may fall in love with a particular detail and want it on every doll you make, despite what the pattern calls for.

DRAGON

There's just something about dragons that floors me every single time I see one in a show or a movie or read about one in a book. They are fantastic! They are beautiful, protective, loyal and just awe-inspiring. My favorite tales are of dragons that are protecting something, be it treasure, a person or a village; I have a special place in my heart for those ones! I designed this teddy bear–style dragon for just that purpose. I hope the dragons you make are loved and tasked with looking after something or someone precious to you!

Materials Needed

- 4.0mm crochet hook (G hook)
- 1 (7-oz [198-g]) skein of medium worsted yarn in light green (I used I Love This Yarn's Light Sage)
- 1 (7-oz [198-g]) skein of medium worsted yarn in brown (I used I Love This Yarn's Toasted Almond)
- 1 pair of 12mm safety eyes
- Fiberfill, for stuffing
- Tapestry needle
- Pins, to hold the limbs in place as you sew
- Scissors

Abbreviations

BLO—crochet only in the back loop of the stitch for the following round

ch—chain

dec—invisible decrease

F/o—fasten off

inc—increase or 2 single crochets in the same stitch

mc—magic circle

sc—single crochet

Head

In light green

Round 1: mc 6. (6)

Round 2: (inc) 6 times. (12)

Round 3: (sc, inc) 6 times. (18)

Round 4: (2 sc, inc) 6 times. (24)

Round 5: (3 sc, inc) 6 times. (30)

Round 6: (4 sc, inc) 6 times. (36)

Rounds 7–12: sc around. (36)

Round 13: (5 sc, inc) 6 times. (42)

Rounds 14–16: sc around. (42)

Insert the eyes between Rounds 12 and 13 with 7 stitches between them. Stuff the head firmly as you decrease.

Round 17: (5 sc, dec) 6 times. (36)

Round 18: (4 sc, dec) 6 times. (30)

Round 19: (3 sc, dec) 6 times. (24)

Round 20: (2 sc, dec) 6 times. (18)

Round 21: (sc, dec) 6 times. (12)

Round 22: (dec) 6 times. (6)

F/o.

Body

In light green

Round 1: mc 6. (6)

Round 2: (inc) 6 times. (12)

Round 3: (sc, inc) 6 times. (18)

Round 4: (2 sc, inc) 6 times. (24)

Round 5: (3 sc, inc) 6 times. (30)

Round 6: (4 sc, inc) 6 times. (36)

Rounds 7–9: sc around. (36)

Round 10: (4 sc, dec) 6 times. (30)

Round 11: sc around. (30)

Round 12: (3 sc, dec) 6 times. (24)

Rounds 13–15: sc around. (24)

Round 16: (2 sc, dec) 6 times. (18)

Round 17: sc around. (18)

F/o, leaving a long tail for sewing.

(continued)

DRAGON (CONTINUED)

Back Legs–Make 2

In light green

Round 1: mc 6. (6)

Round 2: (inc) 6 times. (12)

Round 3: BLO sc around. (12)

Rounds 4–15: sc around. (12)

F/o, leaving a long tail for sewing.

Front Legs–Make 2

In light green

Round 1: mc 6. (6)

Round 2: (sc, inc) 3 times. (9)

Round 3: BLO sc around. (9)

Rounds 4–16: sc around. (9)

F/o, leaving a long tail for sewing.

Muzzle

In light green

Round 1: mc 6. (6)

Round 2: (inc) 6 times. (12)

Round 3: (sc, inc) 6 times. (18)

Round 4: BLO sc around. (18)

Rounds 5–7: sc around. (18)

F/o, leaving a long tail for sewing.

Ears–Make 2

In light green

Round 1: mc 4. (4)

Round 2: (sc, inc) 2 times. (6)

Round 3: (2 sc, inc) 2 times. (8)

Round 4: (3 sc, inc) 2 times. (10)

Round 5: (4 sc, inc) 2 times. (12)

Rounds 6–9: sc around. (12)

Round 10: (dec) 6 times. (6)

F/o, leaving a long tail for sewing.

Wings—Make 2

The wings are made in rows, not rounds. Please read the pattern carefully.

In light green

Row 1: ch 5, turn.

Row 2: Start in the second chain from hook, 4 sc, ch 4 and turn.

Row 3: Start in the second chain from hook, 7 sc, ch 1 and turn.

Row 4: Start in the second chain from hook, 4 sc, ch 4 and turn.

Row 5: Start in the second chain from hook, 7 sc, ch 3 and turn.

Row 6: Start in the second chain from hook, 6 sc, ch 4 and turn.

Row 7: Start in the second chain from hook, 9 sc, do not chain or turn.

Row 8: sc around the top of the wing (you will be creating evenly spaced stitches along this ridge).

F/o, leaving a long tail for sewing.

Horns—Make 2

In brown

Round 1: mc 4. (4)

Round 2: (sc, inc) 2 times. (6)

Round 3: (2 sc, inc) 2 times. (8)

Round 4: (3 sc, inc) 2 times. (10)

Rounds 5–8: sc around. (10)

F/o, leaving a long tail for sewing.

Tail

In light green

Round 1: mc 6. (6)

Round 2: sc around. (6)

Round 3: inc, 5 sc. (7)

Round 4: inc, 6 sc. (8)

Round 5: inc, 7 sc. (9)

Round 6: inc, 8 sc. (10)

Round 7: inc, 9 sc. (11)

Round 8: inc, 10 sc. (12)

Round 9: inc, 11 sc. (13)

Round 10: inc, 12 sc. (14)

Rounds 11–13: sc around. (14)

F/o, leaving a long tail for sewing.

Assembly

Whipstitch the bottom of the head closed. Stuff the body firmly, and sew it to the bottom of the head. Lightly stuff the back feet, making sure the stuffing is just in the foot portion; leave the legs mostly without fluff. Attach 1 leg to each side of the body, making sure your plushie is in a balanced sitting position before finalizing your sewing.

Next, pin the front legs to the sides of your dragon (no need to stuff them). Sew them on once you're happy with their positioning. I like mine positioned in between the back legs so it has a long-armed teddy bear style. Then, stuff the muzzle and attach it to the head between the eyes. Attach the ears to either side of the head. Stuff the horns and sew them on top of the head. Pin the wings to the back and attach them when you are happy with their positioning. Finally, stuff the tail and attach it to the bottom of the back. Use the scissors to cut any leftover yarn tails from all the limbs you've attached. Your Dragon is now done!

GRIFFIN

I absolutely love Griffins—they are such majestic beasts! With the head of an eagle and the body of a lion, they represent courage, pride, strength and grace. They are protectors and fiercely loyal. Did you know that Griffins have one mate throughout their entire life? Legend has it their feathers can restore sight to the blind. Just fascinating! Please enjoy the following pattern and keep in mind what a wondrous creature you are whipping up as you proceed. We use the teddy bear style of assembly here because I find it so endearing.

Materials Needed

- 4.0mm crochet hook (G hook)
- 1 (7-oz [198-g]) skein of medium worsted yarn in white (I used Big Twist's Value White)
- 1 (7-oz [198-g]) skein of medium worsted yarn in brown (I used Red Heart's Super Saver Café Latte)
- 1 (7-oz [198-g]) skein of medium worsted yarn in gold (I used Big Twist's Value Gold)
- 1 pair of 12mm safety eyes
- Fiberfill, for stuffing
- Tapestry needle
- Pins, to hold the limbs in place as you sew
- Scissors

Abbreviations

ch–chain
dec–invisible decrease
F/o–fasten off
inc–increase or 2 single crochets in the same stitch
mc–magic circle
sc–single crochet

Head

In white

Round 1: mc 6. (6)

Round 2: (inc) 6 times. (12)

Round 3: (sc, inc) 6 times. (18)

Round 4: (2 sc, inc) 6 times. (24)

Round 5: (3 sc, inc) 6 times. (30)

Round 6: (4 sc, inc) 6 times. (36)

Rounds 7–12: sc around. (36)

Round 13: (5 sc, inc) 6 times. (42)

Rounds 14–16: sc around. (42)

Insert the eyes between Rounds 12 and 13 with 7 stitches between them. Stuff the head firmly as you decrease.

Round 17: (5 sc, dec) 6 times. (36)

Round 18: (4 sc, dec) 6 times. (30)

Round 19: (3 sc, dec) 6 times. (24)

Round 20: (2 sc, dec) 6 times. (18)

Round 21: (sc, dec) 6 times. (12)

Round 22: (dec) 6 times. (6)

F/o.

Body

In brown

Round 1: mc 6. (6)

Round 2: (inc) 6 times. (12)

Round 3: (sc, inc) 6 times. (18)

Round 4: (2 sc, inc) 6 times. (24)

Round 5: (3 sc, inc) 6 times. (30)

Round 6: (4 sc, inc) 6 times. (36)

Rounds 7–9: sc around. (36)

Round 10: (4 sc, dec) 6 times. (30)

Round 11: sc around. (30)

Round 12: (3 sc, dec) 6 times. (24)

Round 13: sc around. (24)

Change to white

Rounds 14–15: sc around. (24)

Round 16: (2 sc, dec) 6 times. (18)

Round 17: sc around. (18)

F/o, leaving a long tail for sewing.

Back Legs–Make 2

In brown

Round 1: mc 6. (6)

Round 2: (inc) 6 times. (12)

Rounds 3–14: sc around. (12)

F/o, leaving a long tail for sewing.

(continued)

GRIFFIN (CONTINUED)

Front Legs—Make 2

In brown

Round 1: mc 6. (6)

Round 2: (sc, inc) 3 times. (9)

Rounds 3–9: sc around. (9)

Change to white

Rounds 10–15: sc around. (9)

F/o, leaving a long tail for sewing.

Beak

In gold

Round 1: mc 4. (4)

Round 2: (sc, inc) 2 times. (6)

Round 3: (2 sc, inc) 2 times. (8)

Round 4: (3 sc, inc) 2 times. (10)

Round 5: sc around. (10)

F/o, leaving a long tail for sewing.

Tail

In brown

Round 1: mc 6. (6)

Rounds 2–10: sc around. (6)

F/o, leaving a long tail for sewing.

Wings—Make 2

The wings are made in rows, not rounds. Please read the pattern carefully.

In brown

Row 1: ch 5, turn.

Row 2: Start in the second chain from hook, 4 sc, ch 4 and turn.

Row 3: Start in the second chain from hook, 7 sc, ch 1 and turn.

Row 4: Start in the second chain from hook, 4 sc, ch 4 and turn.

Row 5: Start in the second chain from hook, 7 sc, ch 3 and turn.

Row 6: Start in the second chain from hook, 6 sc, ch 4 and turn.

Row 7: Start in the second chain from hook, 9 sc, do not chain or turn.

Row 8: sc around the top of the wing (you will be creating evenly spaced stitches along this ridge).

F/o, leaving a long tail for sewing.

Ears—Make 2

In white

Round 1: mc 4. (4)

Round 2: (sc, inc) 2 times. (6)

Round 3: (2 sc, inc) 2 times. (8)

Round 4: (3 sc, inc) 2 times. (10)

Round 5: (4 sc, inc) 2 times. (12)

Rounds 6–7: sc around. (12)

F/o, leaving a long tail for sewing.

Assembly

Whipstitch the bottom of the head closed. Stuff the body firmly and sew it to the bottom of the head. Lightly stuff the back feet, making sure the stuffing is just in the foot portion; leave the legs mostly without fluff. Attach 1 leg to each side of the body, making sure your plushie is in a balanced sitting position before finalizing your sewing.

Next, pin the front legs to the sides of your Griffin (no need to stuff them). Sew them on once you're happy with their positioning. I like mine positioned in between the back legs so it has a long-armed teddy bear style. Then, stuff the beak and attach it to the head between the eyes. Attach the ears to either side of the head and the wings to the back.

Next, attach the tail to the bottom of the back (no need to stuff it). Use the scissors to cut any leftover yarn tails from the limbs you've attached. Finally, attach a tuft of hair to the end of the tail. I do this by cutting 3 strands of brown yarn, about 4 inches (10 cm) each, and using the latch hook method to attach it to the very tip of the tail. Give the tuft a trim, and when you are happy with its length, your Griffin is done!

PHOENIX

" . . . And from the ashes rose the Phoenix." Everyone knows the powerful legend of the immortal bird whose symbolic reincarnation can be an analogy for many personal struggles that result in growth. Phoenixes are beautiful and represent renewal and rebirth. I found myself reflecting on that as I designed this majestic creature for you . . . and there is a lot of time to reflect while feathering this thing, haha! But good things take time, and I hope you love your finished piece as much as I love mine!

Materials Needed

- 4.0mm crochet hook (G hook)
- 1 (7-oz [198-g]) skein of medium worsted yarn in orange (I used Big Twist's Soft Orange)
- 1 (7-oz [198-g]) skein of medium worsted yarn in gold (I used Big Twist's Soft Gold)
- 1 pair of 12mm safety eyes
- Fiberfill, for stuffing
- Tapestry needle
- Pins, to hold the limbs in place as you sew
- Scissors
- 1 sheet of red felt
- 1 sheet of orange felt
- 1 sheet of yellow felt
- Fabri-Tac glue or hot glue

Abbreviations

dec–invisible decrease
F/o–fasten off
inc–increase or 2 single crochets in the same stitch
mc–magic circle
sc–single crochet

Head

In orange

Round 1: mc 6. (6)

Round 2: (inc) 6 times. (12)

Round 3: (sc, inc) 6 times. (18)

Round 4: (2 sc, inc) 6 times. (24)

Round 5: (3 sc, inc) 6 times. (30)

Round 6: (4 sc, inc) 6 times. (36)

Rounds 7–12: sc around. (36)

Round 13: (5 sc, inc) 6 times. (42)

Rounds 14–16: sc around. (42)

Insert the eyes between Rounds 12 and 13 with 7 stitches between them. Stuff the head firmly as you decrease.

Round 17: (5 sc, dec) 6 times. (36)

Round 18: (4 sc, dec) 6 times. (30)

Round 19: (3 sc, dec) 6 times. (24)

Round 20: (2 sc, dec) 6 times. (18)

Round 21: (sc, dec) 6 times. (12)

Round 22: (dec) 6 times. (6)

F/o.

Body

In orange

Round 1: mc 6. (6)

Round 2: (inc) 6 times. (12)

Round 3: (sc, inc) 6 times. (18)

Round 4: (2 sc, inc) 6 times. (24)

Round 5: (3 sc, inc) 6 times. (30)

Round 6: (4 sc, inc) 6 times. (36)

Rounds 7–9: sc around. (36)

Round 10: (4 sc, dec) 6 times. (30)

Round 11: sc around. (30)

Round 12: (3 sc, dec) 6 times. (24)

Rounds 13–15: sc around. (24)

Round 16: (2 sc, dec) 6 times. (18)

Round 17: sc around. (18)

F/o, leaving a long tail for sewing.

(continued)

PHOENIX (CONTINUED)

Wings—Make 2

In orange

Round 1: mc 6. (6)

Round 2: (inc) 6 times. (12)

Round 3: (sc, inc) 6 times. (18)

Round 4: (2 sc, inc) 6 times. (24)

Round 5: (3 sc, inc) 6 times. (30)

Round 6: (4 sc, inc) 6 times. (36)

Round 7: (5 sc, inc) 6 times. (42)

Fold the piece in half and sc through both sides, around the rounded edge of the wing. (21)

F/o, leaving a long tail for sewing.

Tail

In orange

Round 1: mc 4. (4)

Round 2: (sc, inc) 2 times. (6)

Round 3: (2 sc, inc) 2 times. (8)

Round 4: (3 sc, inc) 2 times. (10)

Round 5: (4 sc, inc) 2 times. (12)

Round 6: (5 sc, inc) 2 times. (14)

Rounds 7–10: sc around. (14)

F/o, leaving a long tail for sewing.

Feet—Make 2

Starting with the first toe, in gold

Round 1: mc 6. (6)

Rounds 2–3: sc around. (6)

F/o.

Second toe

Round 1: mc 6. (6)

Rounds 2–3: sc around. (6)

Do not fasten off; join the next stitch into the first toe, and consider this the first stitch of Round 4.

Round 4: sc around. (12)

Round 5: (dec) 6 times. (6)

F/o, leaving a long tail for sewing.

Beak

In gold

Round 1: mc 4. (4)

Round 2: (sc, inc) 2 times. (6)

Round 3: (2 sc, inc) 2 times. (8)

Round 4: (3 sc, inc) 2 times. (10)

Round 5: sc around. (10)

F/o, leaving a long tail for sewing.

Head Tuft

In orange

Round 1: mc 4. (4)

Round 2: (sc, inc) 2 times. (6)

Round 3: (2 sc, inc) 2 times. (8)

Round 4: (3 sc, inc) 2 times. (10)

Round 5: (4 sc, inc) 2 times. (12)

Rounds 6–8: sc around. (12)

Round 9: (dec) 6 times. (6)

F/o, leaving a long tail for sewing.

Assembly

Whipstitch the bottom of the head closed. Stuff the body firmly and sew it to the bottom of the head. Whipstitch the feet closed (no need to stuff them), and attach them to the bottom of the body, checking the balance as you sew to make sure they are not tipping your plush one way or the other. Next, pin the tail to the lower back; you can use the tail positioning to help balance the doll. Stuff the beak and attach it to the center of the face between the eyes. Attach the head tuft to the top of the head. Use the scissors to cut any leftover yarn tails from all you've attached.

(continued)

PHOENIX (CONTINUED)

Now, we will make all the feathers we need, and actually "feather" the tail before attaching the wings. Begin cutting your feathers; mine each came out to be ¾ x ⅓ inch (2 cm x 8 mm). You will need about 21 red feathers, 26 orange feathers and 35 yellow feathers. Once you have everything cut, begin gluing the feathers to the tail. I started with 3 red feathers on the tip, followed by 3 orange feathers on top of those and finally 5 gold feathers layered on top.

After the tail feathers are glued, you can attach the wings to either side of the body. Once the wings are secured, cut any leftover yarn tails and begin feathering! I started with red on the bottom layer (furthest from the body); it took me about 6 feathers to completely cover the bottom section. Next, glue on orange feathers overlapping the red; it took me about 7 feathers to completely cover this section. Finally, finish off the wing with yellow feathers. I did 2 layers of yellow to make sure all of the orange yarn was covered, which totaled about 10 feathers. Repeat this process with the other wing.

Finally, feather the head tuft! I started by attaching 3 red feathers to the very tip of the front of the tuft. Next, I attached and staggered a layer of orange feathers over the red, which required 4 orange feathers. Lastly, I finished off the bottom layer with yellow feathers, which took 5 feathers. Repeat this process on the back of the head tuft, and when the glue has dried your Phoenix is finished!

HARPY

Harpies are half-woman, half-bird, and they are giant! In mythology, they are monsters that are sent to punish evildoers by snatching them up and taking them to where they will pay for the things they have done. Harpies are often described as hideous creatures . . . but that's not my style! So, I have designed a cuter, chibi version of this monster for you. Get your hook ready, and soon you will have an army of them at your disposal, ready to do you bidding! This pattern is extremely versatile; the color combinations are endless, and you can style the hair any way you'd like.

Materials Needed

- 4.0mm crochet hook (G hook)
- 1 (7-oz [198-g]) skein of medium worsted yarn in preferred skin tone (I used Red Heart's Super Saver Buff)
- 1 (7-oz [198-g]) skein of medium worsted yarn in brown (I used Crafter's Secret's Big Idea Brown)
- 1 (7-oz [198-g]) skein of medium worsted yarn in preferred hair color (I used Caron's Simply Soft Autumn Red)
- 1 pair of 9mm safety eyes
- Fiberfill, for stuffing
- Tapestry needle
- Pins, to hold the limbs in place as you sew
- Scissors
- Fabri-Tac glue or hot glue
- 1 sheet of felt, color depends on your preference for her feathers

Abbreviations

dec–invisible decrease
F/o–fasten off
inc–increase or 2 single crochets in the same stitch
mc–magic circle
sc–single crochet

Head

In preferred skin tone

Round 1: mc 6. (6)

Round 2: (inc) 6 times. (12)

Round 3: (sc, inc) 6 times. (18)

Round 4: (2 sc, inc) 6 times. (24)

Round 5: (3 sc, inc) 6 times. (30)

Round 6: (4 sc, inc) 6 times. (36)

Rounds 7–15: sc around. (36)

Insert the eyes between Rounds 11 and 12 with 6 stitches in between. Start stuffing the head as you decrease.

Round 16: (4 sc, dec) 6 times. (30)

Round 17: (3 sc, dec) 6 times. (24)

Round 18: (2 sc, dec) 6 times. (18)

Round 19: (sc, dec) 6 times. (12)

Round 20: (dec) 6 times. (6)

F/o.

Body

Starting with the first leg, in brown

Round 1: mc 6. (6)

Round 2: (inc) 6 times. (12)

Rounds 3–7: sc around. (12)

F/o.

Second leg

Round 1: mc 6. (6)

Round 2: (inc) 6 times. (12)

Rounds 3–7: sc around. (12)

Do not fasten off; join the next stitch into the first leg, and consider this the first stitch of Round 8.

Rounds 8–10: sc around. (24)

Change to preferred skin tone

Rounds 11–15: sc around. (24)

Round 16: (2 sc, dec) 6 times. (18)

Round 17: sc around. (18)

Round 18: (sc, dec) 6 times. (12)

F/o, leaving a long tail for sewing.

(continued)

HARPY (CONTINUED)

Talons—Make 6

In brown

Round 1: mc 6. (6)

Rounds 2–3: sc around. (6)

F/o, leaving a long tail for sewing.

Wings—Make 2

In red

Round 1: mc 6. (6)

Round 2: (inc) 6 times. (12)

Round 3: (sc, inc) 6 times. (18)

Round 4: (2 sc, inc) 6 times. (24)

Round 5: (3 sc, inc) 6 times. (30)

Round 6: (4 sc, inc) 6 times. (36)

Round 7: (5 sc, inc) 6 times. (42)

Round 8: (6 sc, inc) 6 times. (48)

Fold the piece in half and sc through both sides, around the rounded edge of the wing. (24)

F/o, leaving a long tail for sewing.

Tail

In red

Round 1: mc 4. (4)

Round 2: (sc, inc) 2 times. (6)

Round 3: (2 sc, inc) 2 times. (8)

Round 4: (3 sc, inc) 2 times. (10)

Round 5: (4 sc, inc) 2 times. (12)

Rounds 6–7: sc around. (12)

F/o, leaving a long tail for sewing.

Wig Cap

In red

Round 1: mc 6. (6)

Round 2: (inc) 6 times. (12)

Round 3: (sc, inc) 6 times. (18)

Round 4: (2 sc, inc) 6 times. (24)

Round 5: (3 sc, inc) 6 times. (30)

Round 6: (4 sc, inc) 6 times. (36)

Rounds 7–11: sc around. (36)

F/o, leaving a long tail for sewing.

Hair

To begin making hair similar to the doll that is pictured, first sew the wig cap to the top of the head. Leave any excess yarn from sewing attached; we will use it to attach the strands of hair. If it is not long enough (you need about 10 inches [25 cm]), then cut a new strand of yarn and use it instead. Weave the strand of yarn to the front of the wig cap; this is where we will begin attaching our hair.

Next, cut about 40 strands of red yarn, each about 8 inches (20 cm) long. Begin sewing bundles of them to the wig cap. (I find 4 strands is a perfect thickness for each section.) Keep your sewing line straight, as this will be where the hair parts. Pull your sewing strand very tight every time you secure a hair bundle, and maintain that same tightness as you continue down the wig cap. I usually stop attaching bundles of hair once I get to the back of the head (where attaching the hair would become a vertical task). The last step is to apply a very thin line of glue on each side of the part to make sure the hair doesn't easily come out of the sewn part we just created. Remember: A little bit of glue goes a very long way. Keep the line of glue very thin; we don't want it to bleed through the hair and show. Set the head aside somewhere safe until the glue has dried. Leave the hair strands long for now; trimming is the very last thing we do!

(continued)

HARPY (CONTINUED)

Assembly

Once the glue has dried, whip-stitch the head closed. Stuff the body firmly, and attach it to the bottom of the head. Pin 2 talons to the front of each foot and 1 talon to the back; sew them on (no need to stuff the talons).

Sew the tail to the back of the body, in line with where the color change occurs (no need to stuff the tail). Pin the wings to the back and sew them on. Use the scissors to cut any leftover yarn tails from the limbs you've attached.

Next, we are going to cut a *lot* of tiny feather shapes out of the sheet of felt you selected (about 50!). They should measure ¾ x ⅓ inch (2 cm x 8 mm). We will make our skirt and top out of them, as well as feather the wings and tail. Please use the pictures as reference as to how I layered them. I glued them all directly to the crochet pieces. Take your time, and remember a little glue goes a long way.

Lastly, trim the hair. Take it slow, and only cut a little bit off at a time, because once you go too short, it is really difficult to recover. When you are happy with the length, your Harpy is done!

ONE-EYED, ONE-HORNED, FLYING PURPLE PEOPLE EATER

Materials Needed

- 4.0mm crochet hook (G hook)
- 1 (7-oz [198-g]) skein of medium worsted yarn in purple (I used I Love This Yarn's Neon Purple)
- 1 (7-oz [198-g]) skein of medium worsted yarn in orange (I used Red Heart's Super Saver Pumpkin)
- 1 (7-oz [198-g]) skein of medium worsted yarn in green (I used Caron's Simply Soft Neon Green)
- 18mm safety eye
- Fiberfill, for stuffing
- Tapestry needle
- Pins, to hold the limbs in place as you sew
- Scissors
- 1 sheet of white felt
- 1 sheet of black felt
- 1 sheet of pink felt
- Fabri-Tac glue or hot glue

Abbreviations

ch—chain
dec—invisible decrease
F/o—fasten off
inc—increase or 2 single crochets in the same stitch
mc—magic circle
sc—single crochet

One-Eyed, One-Horned, Flying Purple People Eater! 🎵 That song gets stuck in my head every time I visit this design, and it is also pretty self-explanatory. I hope you enjoy my rendition of this fun monster. I absolutely loved using brighter colors than I normally do when making him—it added so much more whimsy! If you wanted your Purple People Eater to be a bit more scary, you could use more muted tones of the same colors.

Head/Body

In purple

Round 1: mc 6. (6)

Round 2: (inc) 6 times. (12)

Round 3: (sc, inc) 6 times. (18)

Round 4: (2 sc, inc) 6 times. (24)

Round 5: (3 sc, inc) 6 times. (30)

Round 6: (4 sc, inc) 6 times. (36)

Round 7: (5 sc, inc) 6 times. (42)

Round 8: (6 sc, inc) 6 times. (48)

Rounds 9–25: sc around. (48)

Round 26: (6 sc, dec) 6 times. (42)

Round 27: (5 sc, dec) 6 times. (36)

Cut a white felt circle with a diameter of about 1 inch (2.5 cm); cut a small slit in the middle, and insert your safety eye post. This will create the white of the eye. Insert the eye (with its white felt backing) between Rounds 14 and 15. Begin stuffing the body firmly as you continue to decrease.

Round 28: (4 sc, dec) 6 times. (30)

Round 29: (3 sc, dec) 6 times. (24)

Round 30: (2 sc, dec) 6 times. (18)

Round 31: (sc, dec) 6 times. (12)

Round 32: (dec) times. (6)

F/o.

(continued)

ONE-EYED, ONE-HORNED, FLYING PURPLE PEOPLE EATER (CONTINUED)

Feet—Make 2

Starting with the first toe, in purple

Round 1: mc 6. (6)

Round 2: (inc) 6 times. (12)

Rounds 3: sc around. (12)

Rounds 4–7: sc around. (12)

F/o.

Second toe

Round 1: mc 6. (6)

Round 2: (inc) 6 times. (12)

Round 3: sc around. (12)

Rounds 4–7: sc around. (12)

Do not fasten off; join the next stitch into the first toe, and consider this the first stitch of Round 8.

Round 8: sc around. (24)

Round 9: (2 sc, dec) 6 times. (18)

Round 10: sc around. (18)

Round 11: (sc, dec) 6 times. (12)

Begin stuffing the foot firmly as you continue to decrease.

Rounds 12–14: sc around. (12)

Round 15: (dec) 6 times. (6)

F/o, leaving a long tail for sewing.

Horn

In orange

Round 1: mc 4. (4)

Round 2: inc, 3 sc. (5)

Round 3: inc, 4 sc. (6)

Round 4: inc, 5 sc. (7)

Round 5: inc, 6 sc. (8)

Round 6: inc, 7 sc. (9)

Round 7: inc, 8 sc. (10)

Round 8: inc, 9 sc. (11)

Round 9: inc, 10 sc. (12)

Round 10: inc, 11 sc. (13)

Round 11: inc, 12 sc. (14)

Round 12: inc, 13 sc. (15)

Round 13: sc around. (15)

F/o, leaving a long tail for sewing.

Wings—Make 2

The wings are made in rows, not rounds. Please read the pattern carefully.

In green

Row 1: ch 5, turn.

Row 2: Start in the second chain from hook, 4 sc, ch 4 and turn.

Row 3: Start in the second chain from hook, 7 sc, ch 1 and turn.

Row 4: Start in the second chain from hook, 4 sc, ch 4 and turn.

Row 5: Start in the second chain from hook, 7 sc, ch 3 and turn.

Row 6: Start in the second chain from hook, 6 sc, ch 4 and turn.

Row 7: Start in the second chain from hook, 9 sc, do not chain or turn.

Row 8: sc around the top of the wing (you will be creating evenly spaced stitches along this ridge).

F/o, leaving a long tail for sewing.

Assembly

Whipstitch the bottom of the head/body and the feet closed. Pin the feet under the body, making sure he can still sit upright before attaching. When you are happy with their placement, sew them on. Next, stuff the horn and attach it to the top of the head; I began attaching mine right under the magic circle. Then, pin the wings to either side of the body and sew them on. Use the scissors to cut any leftover yarn tails from the limbs you've attached.

Lastly, we will need to make the smile. First, cut a semicircle out of black felt. Mine measured about 1 inch (2.5 cm) wide by ⅔ inch (1.75 cm) tall. Next, cut the tongue out of pink felt. We want the bottom of the tongue and mouth to match, so use the black felt as a template to cut the bottom curve of the tongue. My tongue ended up being 1 inch (2.5 cm) wide and ½ inch (1.3 cm) tall. Glue the pink tongue to the black felt mouth. When it is dry, glue the mouth to the center of the face, under the eye and above the feet. Remember: A little bit of glue goes a very long way! Once your Purple People Eater's mouth is dry and secure, he is done and ready to go!

GARGOYLE

Gargoyles are stunning stone carvings that adorned many medieval cathedrals and castles. Their "grotesque" faces were purposeful and meant to scare away evil spirits. While this gargoyle has more of a sweet demeanor, in my opinion, his job is still the same. Once you whip him up, his mission will be to protect wherever his new home may be!

Materials Needed

- 4.0mm crochet hook (G hook)
- 1 (7-oz [198-g]) skein of medium worsted yarn in grey (I used Caron's One Pound Soft Grey Mix)
- 1 pair of 12mm safety eyes
- Fiberfill, for stuffing
- Tapestry needle
- Pins, to hold the limbs in place as you sew
- Scissors

Abbreviations

ch–chain
dec–invisible decrease
F/o–fasten off
inc–increase or 2 single crochets in the same stitch
mc–magic circle
sc–single crochet

Head

Round 1: mc 6. (6)

Round 2: (inc) 6 times. (12)

Round 3: (sc, inc) 6 times. (18)

Round 4: (2 sc, inc) 6 times. (24)

Round 5: (3 sc, inc) 6 times. (30)

Round 6: (4 sc, inc) 6 times. (36)

Rounds 7–12: sc around. (36)

Round 13: (5 sc, inc) 6 times. (42)

Rounds 14–16: sc around. (42)

Insert the eyes between Rounds 12 and 13 with 7 stitches between them. Stuff the head firmly as you decrease.

Round 17: (5 sc, dec) 6 times. (36)

Round 18: (4 sc, dec) 6 times. (30)

Round 19: (3 sc, dec) 6 times. (24)

Round 20: (2 sc, dec) 6 times. (18)

Round 21: (sc, dec) 6 times. (12)

Round 22: (dec) 6 times. (6)

F/o.

Body

Round 1: mc 6. (6)

Round 2: (inc) 6 times. (12)

Round 3: (sc, inc) 6 times. (18)

Round 4: (2 sc, inc) 6 times. (24)

Round 5: (3 sc, inc) 6 times. (30)

Round 6: (4 sc, inc) 6 times. (36)

Rounds 7–9: sc around. (36)

Round 10: (4 sc, dec) 6 times. (30)

Round 11: sc around. (30)

Round 12: (3 sc, dec) 6 times. (24)

Rounds 13–15: sc around. (24)

Round 16: (2 sc, dec) 6 times. (18)

Round 17: sc around. (18)

F/o, leaving a long tail for sewing.

(continued)

GARGOYLE (CONTINUED)

Haunches–Make 2

Round 1: mc 6. (6)

Round 2: (inc) 6 times. (12)

Round 3: (sc, inc) 6 times. (18)

Rounds 4–8: sc around. (18)

Round 9: (sc, dec) 6 times. (12)

Round 10: (dec) 6 times. (6)

F/o, leaving a long tail for sewing.

Arms–Make 2

Round 1: mc 6. (6)

Round 2: (sc, inc) 3 times. (9)

Rounds 3–14: sc around. (9)

F/o, leaving a long tail for sewing.

Feet–Make 2

Round 1: mc 6. (6)

Round 2: (2 sc, inc) 2 times. (8)

Round 3: (3 sc, inc) 2 times. (10)

Round 4: (4 sc, inc) 2 times. (12)

Rounds 5–6: sc around. (12)

Round 7: (sc, dec) 4 times. (8)

Round 8: (dec) 4 times. (4)

F/o, leaving a long tail for sewing.

Tail

Round 1: mc 6. (6)

Rounds 2–14: sc around. (6)

F/o, leaving a long tail for sewing.

Tail Spike

Round 1: mc 4. (4)

Round 2: inc, 3 sc. (5)

Round 3: inc, 4 sc. (6)

Round 4: inc, 5 sc. (7)

Round 5: inc, 6 sc. (8)

Round 6: inc, 7 sc. (9)

Round 7: inc, 8 sc. (10)

Round 8: (dec) 5 times. (5)

F/o, leaving a long tail for sewing.

Horns–Make 2

Round 1: mc 4. (4)

Round 2: (sc, inc) 2 times. (6)

Round 3: (2 sc, inc) 2 times. (8)

Rounds 4–8: sc around. (8)

F/o, leaving a long tail for sewing.

Ears–Make 2

Round 1: mc 4. (4)

Round 2: (sc, inc) 2 times. (6)

Round 3: (2 sc, inc) 2 times. (8)

Round 4: (3 sc, inc) 2 times. (10)

Round 5: (4 sc, inc) 2 times. (12)

Rounds 6–10: sc around. (12)

F/o, leaving a long tail for sewing.

Wings—Make 2

The wings are made in rows, not rounds. Please read the pattern carefully.

Row 1: ch 5, turn.

Row 2: Start in the second chain from hook, 4 sc, ch 4 and turn.

Row 3: Start in the second chain from hook, 7 sc, ch 1 and turn.

Row 4: Start in the second chain from hook, 4 sc, ch 4 and turn.

Row 5: Start in the second chain from hook, 7 sc, ch 3 and turn.

Row 6: Start in the second chain from hook, 6 sc, ch 4 and turn.

Row 7: Start in the second chain from hook, 9 sc, do not chain or turn.

Row 8: sc around the top of the wing (you will be creating evenly spaced stitches along this ridge).

F/o, leaving a long tail for sewing.

Muzzle

Round 1: mc 6. (6)

Round 2: (inc) 6 times. (12)

Round 3: (sc, inc) 6 times. (18)

Rounds 4–6: sc around. (18)

F/o, leaving a long tail for sewing.

Assembly

First, whipstitch the head closed. Stuff the body very firmly, and attach it to the bottom of the head. Lightly stuff the haunches; we don't want them to be ball-shaped, as we will be sewing an entire "face" of the piece to the body (creating a flat oval instead to look more haunch-shaped). I lightly stuffed them and then flattened them against a surface to show me what they would look like pressed up against the doll when the time came to sew them on. Once you're happy with your haunches' firmness, pin them to either side of the body (make sure the bottom of each is in line with the bottom of the body) and attach.

Now pin the feet right under the haunches and sew them on (no need to stuff them). I sewed mine about 75 percent exposed, 25 percent tucked under the haunches, and made sure my Gargoyle remained balanced while doing so, before finishing them off. Next, attach the arms to the front of the body (no need to stuff them). I sewed them right under where the head and the body join and secured them down the length of the body. I wanted them to stay in place, instead of looking flappy.

Then, pin the muzzle in the middle of the face and sew it on about 75 percent. Stop here and stuff the muzzle firmly. Once you're happy with its firmness, finish sewing it on. Pin the ears to either side of the head and attach (no need to stuff them). Next, lightly stuff the horns and sew them on above the ears. (I started attaching mine about 4 rows from the magic circle on the top of the head.) Pin the wings to the middle of the back and sew them on. Finally, stuff the tail spike and whipstitch it closed. Use that strand of yarn to attach it to the end of the tail, and sew the tail to the plush (no need to stuff the length of the tail). Use the scissors to cut any leftover yarn tails from all the limbs you've attached. With this, your Gargoyle is now finished!

ACKNOWLEDGMENTS

First and foremost, I have to thank my partner, Sergio Rojo. When I accepted this challenge, we had just brought home an eight-week-old puppy, and she was a *very* difficult baby. There were countless nights of little to no sleep, but he owned that so I could rest and design, and write this book. It would *not* have been possible if it wasn't for his support. Not to mention he has been my biggest fan since I picked up a hook, and his enthusiasm while watching me make my dolls and checking out my finished pieces is part of the reason why I love crocheting so much.

Secondly, I have to thank my Instagram friends and beloved testers who supported me the whole way through this. I had to keep these designs secret from the vast majority, and it was really hard, especially when trying to stay motivated, but this amazing group of ladies helped keep the hype up, and I appreciated that so much! These accounts played an intricate role in testing patterns and encouraging my designs: Ella of @nawtjustknots, Abby of @thatssewlacey, Priss of @autumnleavesstitches, Marisa of @monstermancrochet, Kathy of @sewkathycrochets, and Gypsian of @hooksandbookscraft.

I also am *so* thankful to Page Street Publishing for giving me this amazing opportunity! If you had told me when I first started playing with yarn that I would write an amigurumi book, I would have laughed! A specific thanks to Tamara Grasty, who saw my potential and extended me this awesome offer! I will be forever thankful that I was able to create this for the crochet community.

I want to thank my friends and family who have supported my crochet-obsessed lifestyle so enthusiastically; when I say the only time I don't crochet is when I am actively working at my job, sleeping or taking care of my dogs, I mean it. I appreciate that they allow me to do what I feel I *need* to do!

Specifically, I want to thank my grandparents who were so *thrilled* when I first started showing them what I was making when I just began crocheting; it got to the point that if I brought something over to show them when I visited, I wouldn't be leaving with it! My first two Etsy reviews were from my grandpa and my uncle, and I will forever cherish their words. I still remember to this day how excited I was to hear the *cha-ching* of the sales, and how close to tears I was when I saw who bought those listings.

My mom showed me the basic stitches when I first picked up a hook. She went with me to all the craft stores and enabled my yarn-buying habit. My partner, Sergio, protects my yarn from our puppies and dusts and vacuums all the time to keep everything in pristine shape; and he never complains that there is more yarn in this house then the average person may think there should be! My brother, Nick, has the largest collection of my dolls, and he loves each and every thing I make. My friends and coworkers constantly take interest in my crochet and come to visit my booth at events.

Lastly, I want to thank every single person who has bought this book or is holding it in their hands. To anyone who has ever supported me in any way, I am so touched and humbled that anyone would be interested in anything I am doing or making! Please know your support doesn't go unnoticed or unappreciated, and it means more to me than I could ever put into words.

ABOUT
THE AUTHOR

Rikki lives in Hillsboro, Oregon, and has been there her whole life. She has a degree in chemistry; while pursuing her degree, she picked up a crochet hook for the first time. She finished school in 2017 and started working in the tech manufacturing industry a month later. She never put down that hook though!

Rikki runs a crochet business on the side of her full-time job, and she loves to attend conventions to sell her dolls in the artist alleys. It was at conventions that two *Naruto* voice actors (Tom Gibis aka Shikamaru and Brian Donovan aka Rock Lee) purchased her dolls!

Rikki married her high school sweetheart, Sergio, and they are currently raising two puppies together: Bellamy the German shepherd and Bonnie the golden retriever. You can follow them on Instagram if you want to watch their life's adventures unfold at @bellamy.bear.

When Rikki is not crocheting, she's either at work or chasing those dogs around. Otherwise, she's pretty much *always* crocheting! Rikki shares her work on her Instagram @crochetedbyrikki daily, and you can also visit her website crochetedbyrikki.com. When you finish a project from this book, she would love if you'd share your finished project using #creaturesandcryptids on Instagram so you can connect.

INDEX